WHAT THE...

I DID NOT SIGN UP FOR THIS!

**The Ups and Downs
of Supporting an
Entrepreneur**

GABI SPRAKE

ADVANCE PRAISE FOR THE BOOK
AND ITS AUTHOR

Gabi has been supporting her entrepreneurial husband for over 20 years, and she is the first person to write about the journey of supporting an entrepreneur. She has done an exceptional job, and if you are supporting an entrepreneur in any way, this book is absolutely essential to truly understand what it takes.

— Jack Canfield, Coauthor of the *Chicken Soup for the Soul*® series and *The Success Principles*™: *How to Get from Where You Are to Where You Want to Be*

Gabi Sprake possesses an encompassing understanding of commitment, family and love. How she applies these in her book is crisp, clear and illuminating. Her principles of devotional support, insight, persistence and patience are the vehicles that whisked me through this important tome. Gabi's book gives valuable clarity and promise to the spouse that chooses or accepts the supporting role with an entrepreneur. She guides us to discovery of how we can play a supportive role and realize its immeasurable value. As she notes, "Silent doesn't mean weak."

~ Thomas Bähler, author of *Anything is Possible* and *What You Want Wants You*

Brilliant, funny, and full of amazing insights! Gabi Sprake shines a light on what it takes to fully support an entrepreneur through all the ups and downs. This book is a MUST READ for every partner, spouse, family member, friend, and team member who finds themselves playing a key support role to an entrepreneur. Powerfully on-point!

~ Candy Barone, *CEO & Founder of You Empowered Strong*

The support role is often diminished, but this book goes directly to the heart of why some partnerships often fail to reach and exceed the success they are striving for. Gabi Sprake provides deep insight into the challenges we face, and proposes practical yet innovative solutions you can benefit from immediately. Supporting your entrepreneur is a major key to their success.

~ Judy Hoberman, *President, Selling In a Skirt*

Brilliant!! There is no such thing as a successful entrepreneur without someone who provides the wind beneath their wings. Sprake's stories of being that support person are funny, touching and real. A must-read for anyone who lives with or works with an entrepreneur.

~ Monique MacDonald, *Discover Your Sacred Gifts Training and Consulting*

The roller coaster ride can be brutal and scary and knowing how to navigate it is a gift. Being conscious and intentional about your role —the rock and force behind your visionary — is imperative and Gabi Sprake gives you the keys to the castle. Love this book!

~ Shelly Lefkoe, *Co-Founder of The Lefkoe Institute*

Gabi Sprake touches the heart of the matter by showing what it's like to be a spouse, parent, and family that works together to find success and happiness. This is a one-of-a-kind book for entrepreneurs that understands we are more than just our business.

~ Ken Honda, *Bestselling Author*

Every entrepreneur should buy this book for their spouse or partner! Sprake's brilliant, humourous, insightful look into the journey of supporting an entrepreneur is one of the most needed books I have ever read. It is a simple, entertaining read that will shift everyone who reads it.

~ Teresa de Grosbois, #1 International Bestselling author of *Mass Influence*

Editorial Project Management: Karen Rowe, KarenRowe.com

Cover Design: Shake Creative, ShakeTampa.com

Inside Layout: Ljiljana Pavkov

Printed in Canada

ISBN: 978-1-7750157-2-7 (international trade paper edition)

WHAT THE...
I DID NOT SIGN UP FOR THIS!

To my husband Colin, who is truly one of a kind!
Without you, I would never have experienced this life-changing
journey. You are my soul mate and best friend.

To my beautiful daughters Ruby and Jade, thank you for all your
patience and endurance while we built the business. May you
both experience life to the fullest and soak in all of the blessings
that come your way. I am always here to support you.

"Our deepest fear is not that we are inadequate.

Our deepest fear is that we are powerful beyond measure.

It is our light, not our darkness, that most frightens us.

We ask ourselves, 'Who am I to be brilliant, gorgeous, talented, fabulous?' Actually, who are you not to be? You are a child of God.

Your playing small does not serve the world.

There is nothing enlightened about shrinking so that other people won't feel insecure around you.

We are all meant to shine as children do.

It's not just in some of us; it is in everyone.

And as we let our own lights shine, we unconsciously give other people permission to do the same.

As we are liberated from our own fear, our presence automatically liberates others."

MARIANNE WILLIAMSON,
A Return to Love: Reflections on the
Principles of "A Course in Miracles"

Contents

Being Gabi's life partner for more than 20 years and having watched her go through the crazy ups and downs of entrepreneurship, I thought it would be most fitting for me to write the foreword to this incredible labour of love.

In this book, Gabi documents what it is has taken to assist and care for me as I built a global company serving hundreds of thousands of entrepreneurs and their families every year. After years of thinking about writing this book, Gabi decided it was time to assist the unsung heroes who are often forgotten and not acknowledged for everything they do.

This book represents the truth of what it has taken to build multiple million-dollar businesses from the ground up. From eating beans on toast for undetermined periods of time and drinking cheap wine, to eating caviar and sipping expensive champagne and back again—the journey is all here. Gabi has held back nothing, as she wants those of you who are behind the scenes to know you are not alone—and that there is light at the end of the tunnel.

With the world of entrepreneurship exploding, Gabi decided it's time to use her own vulnerability and experience to be of service to others going through the challenges she faced and strategies she used to survive. The biggest challenge is, of course, financial wellbeing. Simply put, when you lack financial stability in your life, this often leads to a lack of confidence in all areas of life. Gabi shares how this situation can best be handled so you—and your marriage—are not in jeopardy.

This book is essential to anyone who is supporting an entrepreneur and who is working hard to achieve massive business and financial success while maintaining a marriage, relationships, family, friends and children.

You are not alone, and neither is your entrepreneur!

Enjoy the read,

Colin Sprake,

Founder and Lead Trainer

Make Your Mark Training and Consulting, Inc.

Acknowledgments

Without my husband Colin's entrepreneurial spirit and drive, this book would have just remained a dream. The idea was conceived five years ago, however nothing had been written until last year—when Colin announced on stage to more than 600 people that my book would be launched within the year and each person would be getting a copy!

I'd also like to acknowledge my parents, Barbara and Hilton, for making me the lady I am today.

Finally, my heartfelt gratitude goes out to all of our Make Your Mark family who believed in me before I believed in myself to get out this book. To those who shared their personal experiences with me, I thank you for your time and transparency.

Preface

I am touched by your interest in reading this book. Before you begin, I'd like to clarify this book is my story—it's about my journey supporting my significant other, Colin's business. Whether you are married, in partnership, or you are paid to support an entrepreneur in a business capacity, this book is for you. This book is **not** a how-to book that claims "follow these ten steps and you'll be able to get through it." It's not about "the top three things you need to do in order to achieve success." It is purely a book about my journey—what has worked for us, and what hasn't.

The book encompasses two eras of my life: one, when I was not in the business and was supporting from the outside while at home with the children, and the second, when I actively joined the business and supported my husband while he grew the company.

It is my hope if you're the significant other of an entrepreneur, (in whatever shape or form that may take), this book may give you peace of mind in demonstrating your journey is quite normal. The book also may show you this role isn't for everyone. It takes a certain person to be an entrepreneur, and I believe it also takes a certain person to play the supporting role behind an entrepreneur.

I'd like to note, as well, the word "spouse" is interchangeable throughout the book for whatever best fits your situation—be it partner, significant other, husband, wife or something entirely different. No matter what you call yourself, you play an important role. Thank you for reading about my journey.

Introduction

Growing up in South Africa, I never would have guessed I would end up half way around the world, running a pole dancing business and living life as the spouse of a successful entrepreneur.

I thought I'd be a plumber.

At least that's what I said in 10th grade, when asked what career I wanted to pursue. I knew plumbers made good money, so I believed it would be a great job. I didn't think about being down in the trenches, amid all the mud and dirt.

I ended up studying to be an esthetician—not what I expected, but completely different than what I ended up doing in my adult life. Who knew that I'd be part-owner of a multi-million-dollar company? That thought never even crossed my mind.

Given the choice, I never would have said I wanted to have a husband who was self-employed, going through risk and reward, stress and sleepless nights. I never would have said I wanted a life where we could have millions today and then lose it all tomorrow. There's no way I would have picked that answer.

But now that I've lived the life, I've come to the realization I was meant to be on this journey. If I weren't, I wouldn't be here. My husband's journey is my journey too; he's learning, but I'm learning in the background.

This is my path as much as his. I wouldn't trade the ups and downs I've been through as the spouse of an entrepreneur for anything. We are where we are because of that wild ride.

The First What the...

The truth is, I said no to this life, more than once. The first time Colin and I met was when he came home to find me in a chair in his lounge. My friend was his roommate at the time and I was over often but he was always traveling in Europe so we hadn't met. The three of us went to dinner that evening and at some point during the night he told my friend, "That's the girl I'm going to marry." She shared this revelation with me later and I laughed out loud. My first reaction was, we have nothing in common, I love being single, I don't know you, I don't want to know you, you aren't even Jewish (which I thought was a big deal for me at the time), so no thanks.

My friend decided to play matchmaker however and told him I was interested. After many requests and just as many rejections, I finally realized he wasn't going to give up. He called me every single day using a myriad of terms of endearment, begging me to go out with him. Finally, after a week of persistence, I decided the best way to get rid of him would be to give in and go on one date then, when it was the disaster I knew it would be, he would take no for an answer.

I was expecting him to be a jerk. In my mind, I had envisioned a quick meal at McDonald's, crude or no conversation, and little else. Then he showed up at the door with a bouquet of beautiful red roses, opened the car door for me, was an absolute gentleman, and took me to the best five-star restaurant in town. He made it really tough for me to say no.

After that date he went away for eight weeks on business and when he returned we had our second date. Then came the third, fourth and so on. Things progressed pretty quickly and after two months, I realized this was the guy I wanted to marry.

This is a running joke between us now. We always laugh about how he gets things quickly and I'm always two months behind. It's been that way with every business we've had. He comes in with a new business idea and it takes me two to six months to get it and fall in love with the idea, just as I did with him.

It was definitely what you'd call a whirlwind romance. We met in South Africa where we both lived at the time. Six months later we were married and then, in another nine months, we moved to Canada. I never thought I'd be in a strange country with no family or friends. It was just the two of us and we had only been together a little over a year. We realized quickly we had to depend on one another more than most couples. We quickly became best friends, and that's been the best thing for us. Basically, our relationship has been one What the... moment after another, and we wouldn't have it any other way.

Make Your Mark – Where We Are Today

We began Make Your Mark in 2009. Make Your Mark is a training business that is the brainchild of my husband, Colin Sprake. He started the business with the goal of helping others to conduct "business with soul," or to do business in a way that comes from a place of caring and is heart-based. In this model, business isn't just about selling, it's about offering products or services that make an impact in the world in a conscious and positive way.

The company is focused on assisting businesses to achieve their full revenue and profit potential by putting in place mindset, sales, marketing and business systems and strategies through seminars, corporate trainings and one-on-one consulting.

The business began with three of us in our basement. Colin and our first employee Cheryl, would pound the pavement to find business, while I'd be in the office taking phone calls, doing spreadsheets, and registering a whopping four people for our first event. Yes, four people. By comparison, we now regularly host events with 200-250 people *every month*. But we started with four.

In 2015, our team grew to include seven members, all while operating out of our 2,500-square-foot basement. Our accountant's advice on moving into a commercial property was: "When you have filled every possible square foot of space with a person and they are beginning to hang out the doors and windows, *then* you move." Although we had some automation and systemization in place, we conducted the majority of the business manually.

Fast forward to 2017. Now we are in an office space of 3,800 square feet, with a team of 22 in the office. Systemization is now a crucial part of the success of the business. We have expanded the company from British Columbia to Alberta and Ontario and added another 40 to our global team. By 2020, we will be at over 400 team members made up of full-time employees and subcontractors as we expand into the United States and Europe. We have over 60,000 members in our database who we've touched in one way or another.

The job I used to do on my own is now managed by three to four people per department. Before we had this luxury and financial ability, I prepared for an event by myself. I created and printed all the handouts, made the name badges, assembled the binders, and did all the set up. That work is all done by between three to five individuals now.

We used to have 15-20 registered in each of our continued learning courses; now we have between 50-100 people per course—and growing rapidly.

Make Your Mark has had a 300 percent growth in revenue over the last three years and grew more than 340 percent in the first quarter of 2017. Before, we were reinvesting all profits back into the business with each expansion, but over the past two years we have achieved the entrepreneurial dream where we are able to have significant profits each year to invest in future plans—or to travel the world enjoying the fruits of our labour.

In the beginning, we had no systems nor processes, and we would change things on the fly. Now, we have systematized every aspect of the company so it can run without a ton of thought involved. In fact, Colin often says, "If you have to think, it's not a system!" As we have grown, we realized we used to be a small little motorboat that could change direction on a dime. Now, we have become a giant freighter, and we cannot quickly change or alter course. In fact, a simple little change has such a huge domino effect it often costs tens of thousands, if not hundreds of thousands.

The scale at which we currently operate, however, is what has made it possible for our business to thrive—and allowed us to finally reap the personal rewards of having made it through the darkness.

What Is an Entrepreneur?

This book is for those who have fallen in love with an entrepreneur—and choose to partner with them as their spouse and support system. Let's establish what I mean when I say "entrepreneur." An entrepreneur is a person who organizes and operates a business, taking on a greater than normal financial risk to do so. They also are known as businessmen, businesswomen, enterprisers, speculators, tycoons, magnates or Mogul dealers, traders, deal-makers, promoters, impresarios, wheeler-dealers, whiz kids, movers and shakers, go-getters, high-flyers and hustlers. To me, it's someone who's got the guts to take the bull by the horns, go against the grain, and set his or her own pace. Entrepreneurs are creative, and they're driven.

> Here's to the crazy ones, the misfits, the rebels, the troublemakers, the round pegs in the square holes... the ones who see things differently — they're not fond of rules... You can quote them, disagree with them, glorify or vilify them, but the only thing you can't do is ignore them because they change things... they push the human race forward, and while some may see them as the crazy ones, we see genius, because the ones who are crazy enough to think that they can change the world, are the ones who do.
>
> – Steve Jobs

Over the years, we have seen a steady upward growth of new business owners. When places hit recession or hard times, people get laid off and many start their own businesses—some rightly so, and others not so much. Those who believe the grass is always greener on the other side—and believe that running a business is going to be easy—are the ones who shouldn't start their own business. Those who believe they should start a business simply because their parents had a business also are the ones who generally shouldn't run their own business.

Just as we all need to take and pass a driving test to ensure that we abide by the rules and keep ourselves and all those around us safe on the roads, so I've always thought people should take a test to determine if they have what it takes to be an entrepreneur—before they risk everything. Colin designed an entrepreneurial test we use in Make Your Mark's Business Mastery program. In it, we ask students to take the test to determine if they have the drive, determination and staying power for the long haul.

In my case, I grew up with a dad who ran a shoe store—and not by his choice. It was his father's shoe store. My dad had studied to be a scientist, graduating with masters. He held a position with a major pharmaceutical company after graduation, and was living his dream. My grandfather, however, wanted help in his store, so he plucked my dad out of his environment and put him in his shoe store. My dad has now been involved with the business for more than 50 years, but he is not an entrepreneur at heart and should never have been one.

There are conscious business owners, and then there are clueless business owners. The conscious ones are aware of what's going on around them; they are action takers who believe in the law of attraction, positive energy and surrounding themselves with like-minded individuals. These entrepreneurs are always striving to better themselves both personally and professionally. They are laser-focused and not afraid of hard work. They are solution-driven, not penalty-focused, and so when life presents them with universal challenges, they seek out assistance to get them over the hurdles instead of giving up.

The business owners who are, for lack of a better word, "unconscious," in my opinion just view entrepreneurship as a pipeline dream or get rich quick scheme. They might make it, or they might not. There's a saying, "Either you do business or you play business." It's the doers who make it; the ones who play are the ones who complain, "This isn't working for me," or "That didn't go my way."

This book is about those who are supporting entrepreneurs serious about achieving exceptional results, and want the freedom and lifestyle a successful business can give them.

What Is the Role of the Spouse?

There is no official definition of an entrepreneur spouse, let alone a manual. However, my definition of an entrepreneur spouse is the person who organizes the life behind the entrepreneur. He or she is someone who can adapt to change, who can go with the flow, who can be spontaneous, can nurture and is strong when needed, and is soft, encouraging, dependable and a good listener. He

WHAT THE... I DID NOT SIGN UP FOR THIS!

or she never takes anything as cast in stone until it's actually cast in stone. An entrepreneur spouse is Superwoman or Superman, basically.

As an entrepreneur spouse, you cannot be a black and white person; you've got to be a rainbow. One thing I've learned about entrepreneurs is they're big dreamers, so they will share big ideas. Maybe they are ideas for right now, maybe they're for tomorrow, or maybe they're for never. I can say from my experience, however, ideas and dreams come true—provided the entrepreneurs put in the work, remain dedicated to their dreams and have the right support system. This is where you come in.

Your Spouse Couldn't Do This without You

I've always preferred being behind the scenes. My spouse is an extrovert, I'm an introvert. At our events, Colin is the master facilitator, the "head chef." He's always been at the front of the room teaching students the ingredients for success, while I was in the back being the "sous chef," or managing all the handouts, name badges and the check-in process. When Colin arrived, he just had to walk in and do his thing. My role was simple— to be of service to the participants, and be aware of and anticipate what everyone needed.

In the beginning, after every event, a student (almost always a female) would say to me, "Wow, thank you for what you do." I'd look at them blankly and say, "I just gave you some handouts and offered you a Kleenex, I didn't do anything." They would clarify, "Thank you for supporting Colin, because with your support you are allowing him to do what he does best. He knows the back of the room is organized, and everyone will get their handouts. Beyond that, he has the mental support and the love that allows him to take time away from the family." It took me a while to let what they were saying sink in.

Students from across the country who I'd never even met before began sending me gifts. Their cards would all be along the lines of, "Thank you for sharing Colin with us for the past four days. We know we're keeping him away from the family." That thought hadn't even occurred to me. What they saw, I never saw. Once they explained to me he couldn't do what he does without me there behind him I realized I play an important role. I realize now for entrepreneurs to be successful, they need to have a strong foundation beneath or beside them. A beautiful spiritualist and energy healer recently clarified what exactly my role has been over the years for Colin. She said "Gabi, you are the light that illuminates his path."

At one point, I felt my contribution to the family would be a financial contribution— that I had to go bring in money to support us. The students made me realize my contribution wasn't meant to be financial. It was supportive— and that was more meaningful a contribution than the former. Interestingly, the emotional support I offered was what allowed him to go out there to bring in the financial support for the family.

If you are the spouse of an entrepreneur, do not diminish your role as a support person. Even if you're not involved in the business and are instead at home managing the household—keeping the home clean, feeding, bathing and putting the kids to bed, or putting dinner on the table—your role is critical to the entrepreneur. Whether your spouse is embarking on a new business venture or an established one, they are dealing with constant changes. For your spouse to come home to a stable environment where he or she can just relax and not have to "run" everything takes a huge amount of stress off his or her plate.

Colin always asks students at the end of all our events to return home and look those in the eyes who allowed them to be at the event that day. It could be their child, spouse, partner, colleague, sitter, or whoever—but, please, offer them gratitude.

This book is for you if...

This book will best serve those who support entrepreneur spouses. Chances are, you want to live a secure, stable, worry-free lifestyle—perhaps like you used to before your spouse started a business. Instead, you're having a hard time seeing the vacation your spouse talks about, when all you see is the backyard. You dream of the day you don't have to think, "Can I afford this right now?" and you long for the day you can give your kids everything they desire and deserve.

You may feel overwhelmed with trying to keep your family's home life afloat while your spouse toils away at the business. You support the emotional and home needs for the family, and perhaps you even support the business itself as part of the team. But the bottom line is, you're burnt out and near your breaking point for how much longer you can play the support role. You need a support system of your own right now.

That's where this book comes in. Colin and I have run the gamut of emotional highs and lows of running a business, while trying to maintain a healthy and happy marriage and family life. It's certainly not always easy, but I can assure you it's worth the effort. If you want to learn about our own breaking points and how we managed to stay afloat emotionally and financially, read on. We know you can make it, too.

Chapter One

Before We Hit the Mark

> *"Strength and growth come only through*
> *continuous effort and struggle"*
> ~ NAPOLEON HILL

I'll never forget the day I had to go to my daughters' private school and say, "I can't afford school fees. What can I do to keep my children here?" This was one of the hardest and most humbling things I have ever had to do. With my pride in my pocket, I offered to scrub toilets, drive every field trip and serve every hot lunch if I needed to in order to keep them in that school.

For about two years, my daughters were able to attend at a heavily reduced rate. They never knew about it; we never told anyone. It was too embarrassing to say, "Yes, we have a business but yet we can't afford school fees." There was much shame and humiliation in not being able to afford things for the family.

Another day that will remain in my memory was when I was driving my 4- and 6-year-old children home one day.

We approached an intersection with a McDonalds and a grocery store. My girls said, "Can we have McDonalds? Please Mom, please Mom, can we?" I had $10 in my wallet, and that's all I had to my name. I felt bad; I couldn't even treat my kids to a McDonalds Happy Meal.

I decided to be straightforward with my kids. I said, "Girls, here's the deal. I have $10. We can go to McDonalds, and I can buy you a treat. It would be fun, you would get the toy and you'd get to eat right now. Or, we could take the same $10 and go to the grocery store, where I can buy food to feed you for the week. Which choice should we make?" The 6-year-old said, "I'd like to eat for the week." I told her, "Great! So right now, there's no treat. The opportunity will come back, but right now we have to make the better choice to go buy food that can last for the week."

It was times like those when I thought, "I might have signed up to support my spouse, but I didn't necessarily sign up for this." Yet, I kept on thinking back to my mom. She always said to me, "Even if you have nothing else, if you have love in a family and a marriage, it will get you through anything." I'd remember, I just needed to keep the faith and trust in my spouse.

It Feels Like It's All Their Fault

If you're married to an entrepreneur, it may feel like everything is his or her fault—maybe an unhappy marriage or an empty bank account. "If my spouse would just get a job," you may think, "we wouldn't be dealing with the problems we're dealing with."

I feel your pain. I've been there. You're tired from all the ups and downs. It might be feast or famine. When things are great and business is coming in, your spouse is excited. As soon as things are not so great, you've got a whole different beast walking around. You're never quite guaranteed who is going to walk in the door that evening, or what kind of temperament he or she is going to be in — and those emotions will get projected onto you.

The state you're in may or may not be what you signed up for. You may have married someone who was employed, working for someone else. But you're here now. You're on the roller coaster and you have to learn to just ride the wave — the good, the bad and the ugly.

Like my mother taught me, I had to learn to trust. It takes time to build a business, and it takes patience. I had to put my trust in my partner and say, "I trust you to go and do what you do." I saw his hard-working nature. He was never lazy; he was a go-getter, always on the ball with what needed to be done. I saw his optimism and I couldn't crush that passion. Instead of expressing my fear, I said, "I believe in you. You've got two kids to feed. I put my faith and trust in you to provide for the family, so go do what you do and I'll do what I do here. We had a deal that I stay home with the kids, so I need you to go fulfill your deal now. I'll be here to support you."

We owned our own home at the time when Colin decided to leave his good-paying job. To prepare for unknown times ahead, we decided to buy a townhouse to downsize the mortgage in case money didn't come in as quickly as before. We downsized our entire lifestyle, to be able to accommodate building a new business.

A Pole Lot of Fun

Colin gave up his role as CEO of a mining equipment company in November 2004. He parted ways to go into business to build Make Your Mark from the ground up. Instead, he went to a convention and came home saying, "I found this fantastic idea. I'm going to be a partner in a pole dance company!" I said, "What convention were you at and what the hell were you doing there?" I thought it was a stripper convention. He says "No, no, no, it's a great idea! The founder needs the financial backing. Can we back her?"

I thought, "Are you crazy?" Instead, I said, "We made our deal. You be the bread winner. I have to support you. This business doesn't sit well with me, but just go make money. Go feed your family." So we began a pole dancing business. To help launch the company, Colin asked me to hold a marketing party at the house. He said, "I want you to bring your friends." My response was, "I don't have too many friends and I'd like to keep them!" I ended up just inviting one girlfriend (I felt it safe to sacrifice just one!)

but we had so much fun! I fell in love with the concept. I recognized the business had great potential.

And it did—we basically went from zero to hero overnight. The business grew and we did phenomenal; we made millions in six months. It became the biggest home pole dancing business in Canada. Then, we brought it to the United States. We went to Australia. We went to the U.K. We went to South Africa. The company was all the rage. We were in newspapers, magazines and TV shows in the United States, and it was incredible.

The company's success continued for quite a while. We lived the high life, buying fancy cars and what not. But all along we knew it was a fad; it was the new trend and at some point it was going to change.

The Next Big Thing

Ultimately, we only changed businesses because our team was asking for more. They realized, "Okay, I get paid $300 for each party, then I leave and that's it. I might get a call back, I might not. But, if I sold them something, I would get residual income." So we thought, "What can we do to create residual income for our business owners? How can we sell them something to continue that feeling of empowerment?" We came up with the idea if you're feeling beautiful on the inside, you may also want to feel beautiful on the outside. Pole dancing worked on the inside, but what could work on the outside?

Skincare became a good option because it was related to women's growth, feelings and emotions. The parties were enhanced by pampering the hostess with a hand and foot treatment, all the while educating the ladies in our skincare. I had studied to be an aesthetician, so this add-on was easy and comfortable for me.

We didn't charge any more for our parties with this addition, but instead offered that if you bought $30 worth of skincare, you pole danced for free. If you didn't buy skincare, then you still paid for your pole dancing. The majority of guests would make a purchase, and then the "fun" really began as I spent the next two hours teaching them pole dancing.

Before we started with the spa company, I was against going into skincare. I had worked in the industry, and was aware of the competition. But you can't stop a bull in the china store, and Colin was determined to move forward with the idea. So, we changed the "Pole Lot of Fun" party theme to "Spa Lot of Fun."

The cost of the skincare inventory is what killed us. The products were all organic and natural— green tea, lavender fragrances. They were beautiful products, and it was successful at first. Our biggest clientele came from the United States, and then Canada. But then the 2008 Recession happened, and Americans quit buying. Canadians continued buying, but not at the rate we needed to survive as a company. We ended up with a garage full of $500,000 worth of skincare that wasn't going anywhere.

I was against going into skincare. I had worked in the industry, and was aware of the competition. But you can't stop a bull in the china store, and Colin was determined to move forward with the idea.

Popcorn Confessional

Several months passed before Colin said to me, "The skincare products have an expiration date. We need to move our inventory. Let's create gift baskets!" I said, "What?" He replies, "I'll show you. He built a basket with all the skincare products and said, See? We will approach executives in different companies. They can buy Christmas spa baskets from us with skincare products in them, and candles and music."

So he built the gift baskets, and he sent me out to sell them. Not too sure where to start, I approached my warm leads first. I went to my dentist, and he said he couldn't help me, but he gave me a phone book of all dental specialists who buy Christmas gifts for dentists. I went door to door and sold gift baskets. I would go into offices and place my most high-end basket on the receptionists' counters. Their expressions were all the same – eyes widened, faces lit up and they always asked, "Is this for us?" My response was, "No, but it could be!" The first year, we made more than $10,000. Not bad, we thought, for a two-month seasonal business.

The following October, we switched things up and sold gourmet food baskets. Colin would build them, and I'd go out and sell them. It grew slowly, but then in the third year, we hit the jackpot. I went into one orthodontist's office, and he ordered 150 gift baskets, which helped the business skyrocket.

However, the orthodontist would only place the order if we reduced the price. Being a true entrepreneur, Colin said, "Yes, we'll take the order and, yes, we'll give you the price that you want." The downside to this was I had to outsource different foods to put into our gourmet food gift baskets. I couldn't shop at my normal, gourmet wholesalers, as it wouldn't work with the price we'd quoted him.

Through the gift basket business, I had made friends with one of the food managers at the local Walmart. During this time, she called me to say, "I've got this great special. It's a large bag of caramel popcorn for only $1!"

To me, a $1 bag of popcorn was a huge deal—we needed it to get down costs on those 150 baskets. I went into Walmart, looking like a deranged woman who was going to get the best deal of a lifetime. Since the popcorn was on special, it was at the front of the aisles so people could see it from all different angles—and they could see me, taking popcorn off the shelves not just one by one, but by putting my arm at one end of the shelf and moving it across the entire shelf, cleaning all the bags off the shelf in one fell swoop and piling them up into my cart. At one point, I noticed a woman watching me. I'm sure she was thinking, "What the heck is she doing?" But she saw the price and said, "What a great deal."

Of course, she had no idea this deal was vital for me. All she saw was this crazed woman buying cartloads of popcorn, so therefore it must be a great deal. So she started taking popcorn off the shelf. I never in my life thought I'd come so close to punching someone over a bag of popcorn. It felt like she was taking away my gold.

I'm not a confrontational person, but I actually said to her, "Excuse me, can you please leave this popcorn alone. It's mine." She must have thought I was on drugs. By then, we had created a bit of a scene, so the manager came up and said, "Don't worry, Gabi, I've got boxes prepared for you and set aside." I could have apologized to the lady, but instead I turned to her with a sneer on my face and walked away smugly with the manager to go get my pre-packaged boxes.

At the time it was a serious situation for me, but it's now quite funny to recall how ridiculous I must have looked. I certainly hadn't signed up for *this*! But of course, desperate times call for desperate measures.

A Bleeding Business

Although the gift baskets produced reasonable income, our profits were all going back into the skincare company, which was continuing to fail. Before Colin quit his job, we had owned 13 rental properties. We sold them all bit by bit and put that money into the skincare business, which was millions of dollars. Once all the rentals were gone, we started to borrow money from friends.

We shouldn't have tried to keep a bleeding business going; we were just finding a bigger and bigger Band-Aid. But Colin was emotionally involved. He was determined to make it work, so we'd borrow more money. For many months I would sit quietly and visualize all the inventory in my garage being taken way. I would picture the truck reversing into the driveway, I'd smell the fumes from the exhaust and I could hear the beeping sound of the reverse lights.

Finally, we ended up liquidating the business. My visualization became reality. The truck came to pick up the skincare products, just as I had seen, smelled and heard it in my mind. It was a glorious day for me; I stood there smiling from ear to ear because the noose was now gone. But as I turned toward Colin to celebrate that joyous moment, I noticed he wasn't sharing the same emotions. He was in tears. He was deflated and devastated. His "baby" hadn't survived and he was mourning his loss. It was one of the hardest days of his life. We didn't realize at the time this experience and education would lead him to our next adventure.

Without the skincare company to worry about, we decided to go back to Make Your Mark. The business had been born in 2004, but we hadn't done much with it yet. Colin wanted to do something around business and coaching, but didn't yet know quite what.

We Finally Hit the Mark

Colin ended up putting an advertisement on Kijiji, an on-line classified site in Canada, saying he'd give entrepreneurs a three-hour consultation—a bird's eye view into their business. He listed his phone number, and three days later he got a call. He didn't have a clear plan yet, he just knew he was going to sell something. The prospect said, "Can I hire you?" And he said, "Yes, you can hire me." Then he put down the phone and said, "Oh my God. What do I do now?" Make Your Mark had officially begun, as a consulting business. That woman has been a client of ours ever since. Now eight years later, her daughter is part of our program.

The best way to market your business is to get out there and be seen.

Colin began going to every networking group he could to promote our first Make Your Mark event, and that's how the company grew. He would attend at least two to four events per week, building relationships everywhere he went. Slowly, it went from two people, to three, to four for our first seminar. The cost to attend was $100 each— and the room rental alone was $500! Even though we were financially behind that day, we also were excited and grateful. It was times like these when Colin's drive and commitment kept him focused and even more determined to succeed. Thankfully, that was just the starting point of great growth.

Chapter Two

Out with the Old, in with the New

"Go as far as you can see; when you get there, you'll be able to see further."
~ Thomas Carlyle

As the Business Grew, I Grew

As I first adjusted to life as the wife of an entrepreneur, I felt the Gabi who I'd known had died—I didn't know who I was anymore. I had two young children, a husband, and a house to take care of while he grew the pole dancing business. My life had changed so much, that I was trying to find myself again.

Meanwhile, at the pole dancing parties, these women would come in and I would think, "Oh, look! There's me walking in the door!" They would walk in round-shouldered, scared, self-conscious and not too sure about the evening. They would share how they weren't feeling feminine; they were just living day to day, raising kids, taking care of their husbands, and managing the drudgery of their routine.

Then by the end of the evening, some of them were floating. It was like watching butterflies morph from a bland worm into a radiant beauty. They were confident, and you could actually see a renewed strength in them. Most of them had come alive, reawakened from within. They left feeling sexy and empowered and feminine and good about themselves and I thought, "Wow. This business just changed someone's life."

It was incredible to see the transformation of someone walking in with the weight of her new life on her shoulders, and walking out going, "I had forgotten, I'm a woman inside! And I've got a life of my own, and I can have fun!" At least, that was my perception of what they were feeling, because I was feeling likewise.

I was only 33, and I had this entirely new support role as wife of an entrepreneur and mother. The pole dancing business helped me get through those times when I was feeling, "Where have I gone, who am I, and where am I?" I didn't have many girlfriends at the time because we had just left our country and I was too fearful to make new friends in Canada. Hosting pole dancing parties became a wonderful way for me to get out there, meet people and have fun. I'd go home with the same laughter as the ladies at the party. Never mind them having a good time, I was having an amazing experience. Therefore, I went from "Are you crazy?" when Colin first told me about the business idea to "This is pretty cool. I can get into this."

The business ended up assisting my personal life, physically and mentally. Physically, I was becoming fit, and mentally I was feeling good about myself. I was feeling feminine, and laughing so much more. Even though I entered the business in support of Colin, what I got from it I believe was actually greater than what he got.

When you sign up to support your partner, you don't quite know what the journey will be like. But I can say with every one of his businesses, I have grown. As soon as my husband began the business, I had to take off my blinders. When I did, I realized the whole physical fitness factor behind the sport. It awakened a new respect in me for professional dancers, as I experienced just how much work went into it. Pole dancing was no walk in the park, it was work!

The key to the success of the business was Colin's drive. He had a vision from the start of what pole dancing would do for women, without even being a woman, and he was great at getting the business into the media. We became the biggest home pole dancing company in the world. Later, pole dancing studios began to pop up. They weren't around at the time we were doing home parties; we had figured people would prefer to come to a home, in a safer environment. But women started going to the studios for the fitness side of the dance. Our parties met the empowerment, feminine and fun aspects of the dance, while the studios focused on fitness.

I Bring the Pole... You Bring Your Girlfriends

Most people are curious about how the pole dance company worked, so I figure you may be, too. Here's the scoop: If someone called us up and said they wanted to host a party, I'd explain the process as such:

"I will come to your house for two hours. The cost is $30 per lady. I bring the pole, you bring your girlfriends and together we'll make a 'pole lot of fun.' I will bring music and some boas, and you are responsible for setting the scene—light some candles, and dim the lighting because people get self-conscious in bright lighting. Dress comfortably, with no skirts because we're going to be on the floor. We can have a glass or two of courage—but no getting sloshed.

"And there will be rules. If any of your girlfriends are totally inebriated, they won't be allowed to be on the pole because there is a danger factor to it. They can pull it down, and it can crash. I will teach you five or six pole dance moves, then we'll put them together to do a little routine."

I'd begin the evening by introducing them to the pole. I'd say, "Personally, I call him Brad. This is my Brad Pitt. For tonight he can be whoever you'd like him to be." Sometimes they would change the name. One party was the funniest—I said, "Ladies, I'd like you to meet Brad," and this woman behind me goes, "Oh no, that's Brenda." I was like, "Okay, Brad or Brenda, whatever your preference is, I'm good with it."

We did bring a little sexual energy, but all in good, clean fun. I'd tell the room, "Brad is the best dance partner you'll ever have, and he won't step on your toes." Everyone signed a waiver beforehand so they wouldn't sue us if the pole came down, which happened when some women didn't obey the rules and jumped on the pole. Then we put on the boas, they picked their music and that's when I saw them come alive. Some of them were like, "Oh my god. This feels brilliant!" while others were stiff and awkward.

I found the girls in their 20s who would come to parties were the ones who wanted to wear the fishnet tights, high-heel shoes and act sexual. Then when it came to actually dancing on the pole, they would crumble because they had no self-confidence.

My 30-year-olds were new moms trying to find themselves; they forgot who they were, and were looking to be empowered, and to feel feminine and alive again. They were shy at the start, but eventually came out of their shells and weren't as self-conscious anymore.

Women 40 and older were my favorite. They came with the mindset and attitude of "I'm going to have fun, I don't care what you think about me. This is my night, and I'm going to do what I want." I could see the different maturity levels come through. The crème de la crème were my 70-year-olds who had nothing to prove and were amazing! I did a party for the Red Hat Society. That was the wildest party I held. It was a burlesque evening, and they all came dressed to the nines. They were crawling around on the floor, spanking each other's backsides and having fun. It was the best party I'd ever had.

No matter the age group at the party, one thing I told everyone was what I often told myself—you'll enjoy the experience more if you just let go. Don't hold back.

Two Feet In

Just like at the pole dancing parties, one thing I learned about being the spouse of an entrepreneur is if you're in, you're in. I've heard divorced people speak regrettably about their marriage, "Never mind two feet in, or even a big toe. I was zero feet in."

> *To be successful in marriage and in business, you need to be fully committed.*

Are you two feet in, as the spouse of an entrepreneur? The role requires full, not half-hearted, support. If you're not, the relationship and/or the business will dissolve. The road ahead will be rocky, and you must be emotionally prepared for it.

Chapter Three

Know When to Cut Your Losses

> *"When you are pushing the boundaries,*
> *mistakes are inevitable.*
> *How you react is important."*
> ~ RICHARD BRANSON

The Most Expensive Garage in the Neighbourhood

The pole dancing business was a success; our subsequent skincare business was a different story. The lesson was: Learn when to cut your losses. For a long time, we kept on going into debt to get nowhere. We started with $100,000 in debt against the house, then it became another $100,000 with a loan from a friend. When it became an additional $100,000 in debt owed to creditors, that's when we hit our breaking point.

We had the most expensive garage in the neighbor-hood—lined with skincare products piled up high that weren't selling. Our car got more bashed and buckled every day, because every time we tried to get out the door, it would hit boxes of inventory. You can't use $400,000 worth of skincare on yourself. Or your mom. We couldn't give it away quickly enough.

We got rid of quite a bit of product through the gift basket business, but we realized the only way to really get rid of it was to jump ship. It was a tough phone call for Colin to make, because of all the time we spent getting it branded. He'd spent time with the labs creating formulas and scents, and we had made our own labels. We went to a packaging facility in Kelowna, B.C. for the bottling and packaging. It was our baby. It was us.

It was a sad day for Colin because it was the end of his dream as he knew it. Our investment was nowhere near the return we got; we had spent $400,000 and got back $20,000! It was a huge and bitter pill to swallow, but we had to have that death and burial to be able to move on to our next adventure.

Failures are Learning Opportunities

When Colin signed away the product, he called it a death certificate. His dreams were driving out from the complex. What he saw as a death, I saw as a rebirth, or a new beginning. I was sensitive to his needs, but I could really see that now we could move on and put all that stress behind us. But he was devastated; to him that was his first failure, and he didn't know how to handle it. To any entrepreneur, there's a first success and a first failure.

From there, Colin went through a slump until he was ready to say, "Alright, let's put on our big boy pants again and keep on going. How do we fix this? Let's find a solution." That's when he determined, "Let's go back to my original Make Your Mark brand. Let's revive that and go for it."

The beautiful part behind the skincare experience was that now he could help other entrepreneurs who were feeding a company going downhill. He could see the big picture and tell them, "You know what guys, it's time to pull the plug. Take it off life support, because you're not going to revive it." He was able to relate to others going through that experience, because he'd been through that emotional attachment himself.

In the end, Colin came to realize the skincare business didn't fail. It taught him success is like that famous Winston Churchill quote, 'going from failure to failure without loss of enthusiasm.' And the other lesson is that he was given the experience to be able to coach others.

At times like that, remember failure is an event, not a person. That's a distinction. If you look at the definition of failure, it's just that the outcome wasn't how you had intended it. Failure is in fact a learning experience.

We call our losses our education fund, because they're investments in life lessons. Did the skincare lesson cost a lot? Yes. Could it have cost more? Oh yes.

The Business May Not be the Only Loss You Have to Cut

After accepting the fateful end of our skincare business, we moved to, "What business are we going to start next?" At that point Colin knew he would always be an entrepreneur and never even considered going back to a full-time job. But for some of you who have just gone through the same experience of a failed business, now would be the time to make some serious decisions—especially if you have a family that depends on you. You may need to get a traditional job. Perhaps that just means working part-time or taking various side jobs until you get another business off the ground.

In our case, we had income coming in, it just wasn't anywhere near what we needed to cover all the extra debt we'd taken on. Colin could have gone back to his mining career and made a lot of money again, but we were not bleeding enough for him to make that decision. Instead, Colin decided he was going to cut his losses and find part-time work. At one point he asked a friend of ours who had a catering company, "Can I come and assist you on the weekends?" The guy paid him pennies, but Colin showed humility. The nice part was that Colin would often be given a few bottles of top shelf wine, which we had grown so accustomed to drinking when the pole dancing business was flying high. Savoring each sip took us back to those days when we did not care about spending $50 or $100 on a bottle of wine. Now, we were buying cheap wine and making a bottle last an entire week.

At the same time, we had a huge lawsuit laid on us by two ladies from the United States about the pole dancing business. They were upset we had changed the business from a franchise structure to a network marketing structure. They also didn't want to sell skin care. Our biggest learning lesson here was that we made a significant change without consulting the entire data base and asking them what type of product they would like to sell. We approached only three of our top territory owners and discussed the skin care with them. They all loved the idea and saw the big picture of making residual income. They were fully on board. With our market research from only those three people, we went ahead and changed everything to the new structure and then informed the business owners. For the most part many of the owners liked the idea, some loved it and unfortunately others detested it. With this particular group of owners, they became upset and vocal and so Colin did his utmost to work with them in setting up a repayment structure to show goodwill. Our lawyers at the time were of a different mindset and advised us to shut the company and walk away instead of paying them back. Because one of our core values is integrity, that did not sit well with Colin and he went out and incurred more debt to pay them back as much as we could. It was important to him that he could put his head on the pillow at night knowing he had done the right thing.

That situation compounded the stress on Colin, as he had never experienced a lawsuit and it was attacking his integrity. I can say it was the worst time of our lives. I have never seen Colin so down, negative, broken, and full of fear. We would have police sirens go off and Colin would think they were coming for him – it's crazy how the mind works and makes you feel guilty even though you know you have done nothing wrong.

Colin now has a statement that we live by when doing marketing; when you are fishing, instead of wondering if the fish will like what you put out as bait, dive into the water and ask them what they would like! If only we had done that with the skin care business, it may have taken a whole new road instead.

Thankfully, Colin started reading books to get his mindset back on track. He sought out the most powerful lawyer through one of his friends in California and they were able to squash the case. In fact, the ladies phoned begging him not to go through with the counter-lawsuit. It sure was a tough end to 2008.

Tough times indeed, but we weren't starving. We just had to change the way we spent money. For example, in December 2008 Colin bought me a Garmin GPS for Christmas. They had just been released onto the market and therefore came with the price tag of $500. He was so excited to give it to me, however as I opened it, my face dropped and my inside voice couldn't contain itself, "Are you kidding me? We can't afford this." My logical brain had done the math and this had to be returned. This was another crushing moment for my budding entrepreneur, as I returned the device and spent the money on groceries and necessities instead. All he had wanted to do was treat me to something nice, but unfortunately the timing wasn't right.

We had to change our mindset in order to get through that stage. If we had continued with the lavish lifestyle we'd become accustomed to, we would have gone broke. Were these easy choices? No. But for survival, we did what we had to do. I've come across entrepreneurs who have no money to feed their kids. That's when I say, "Go and get a job. Quit playing around now and just go get a job."

> There comes a time when you need to paint your spouse a clear picture that right now, he or she needs to take baby steps to build the business. Entrepreneurs need to understand their choices; their dreams and their visions of the pot of gold will have consequences and an impact on the family.

At Make Your Mark, when we have a new student join our Sherpa program and they are just in the infancy stage of their business and still working a full time job, Colin and I highly recommend they keep their day jobs until they are generating income in the new venture. Then, and only then, do we encourage them to leave their job and focus 100% on their new business. This can be a much slower pace for many entrepreneurs, however it's the least stressful when considering your family's well-being and happiness.

Stay Focused on Family, or You May Lose That Too

Because of the intense and unstable situation entrepreneurship presents, some spouses just don't hang around. Couples don't always realize the distance that's been created between them. Neither side is making an effort, or one side is making an effort, but the other is not.

I grew up with a dad who worked 24/7. He devoted his life to his shoe store and consequently my parents did not have a happily-ever-after marriage. Their situation taught me first-hand how easily we can devote ourselves to a passion without realizing the damage being done to the family life. So when Colin said to me, "I want to devote my life to my work," I thought, *sure, go ahead*, because that's all I know. But, I remembered my parents' situation and became aware of not following in their footsteps. I thank my parents for enduring that learning lesson as I too could have gone down that same route. When Colin worked with the mining company, he traveled for six to eleven months of the year, so I became accustomed to a man who was never there. He was so determined to devote his life to having a successful business that at one point he didn't even want children—he believed children would slow him down and be a hindrance to achieving success. It took us about three years to finally make the decision to have children. He's certainly glad we did—he loves our girls and has no regrets. In fact, he never really has been slowed down by the kids, because I've always taken care of the girls and him. As a result, he was able to focus on the business.

For the first three years of our oldest daughter's life, I was essentially a single parent. It was tough, because Colin would pop into my life for a while, and then pop out again. But when our second child was 18-months old, he said, "I can't travel anymore. The kids are growing up and I'm missing out on their first words, their first steps, their first everything."

What he didn't anticipate was the amount of time away from home being an entrepreneur would require as well. If a business owner is devoted to work, he or she is hardly present at home. However, Colin has been cognizant of families falling apart because of the work stress and the long hours, so he pushes for family time.

We have seen how important it is for couples to build their schedules around the family. Now, we schedule family vacations first. At the same time, if work creeps in, sometimes you need to be flexible. Entrepreneurs change their minds so much, the support structure has to be able to go with that flow.

If we have to make changes, we sit down with the kids and tell them, "Mom and Dad are working for you guys so we can go away and have these vacations, or so you can have a new iPhone, or anything else you desire. If you want something, we have to work. We're working for you, not for us, to make a contribution to the family."

My daughter had to go to Finland for gymnastics two years ago, which was a $20,000 trip. We explained, "Honey, trips like that don't just happen. You have to work hard for it." We explain to them the reasoning behind all the hard work, so they know we are not trying to ignore them or push them aside; there are rewards that come with hard work.

Over the years we have found a solution to balance the family and work life. On our first family trip to Mexico when the kids were young, Colin would get up every day at 5 a.m. and work until 9 a.m. The children and I love to sleep in so it worked perfectly for all of us. He would attend to work while we slept, and the girls weren't even aware that he was doing this. Once they were awake, we would spend the day together having quality time and no one felt left out. This worked so well we continued this at home and on weekends. Now, should Colin have anything pressing to get done, he follows the same procedure and everyone is happy.

Being an entrepreneur and having a family is not for every personality type. I know that if I had my own separate business, I would dedicate my life to it, and it would cost me my family. I first realized this when I started working in the business with Colin. I'd be doing accounting when dinner was ready and I'd say, "I'll come as soon as I get my books done." I'm single-focused when I want to be. I wouldn't know when to stop. Colin has more discipline than me. Know which personality type you are. Perhaps, like me, you're meant to support the entrepreneur rather than be one yourself.

I'd like to close this chapter by sharing a story from our clients, Janice and Doug Friesen from TAK Logistics. Doug has been involved in Make Your Mark since attending one of our events in 2011. Janice attended our Business Mastery course in 2016 and now volunteers for us at many events.

CASE STUDY:
Janice Friesen, TAK Logistics Inc.

Our story: My entrepreneur went from a secure position with the Canadian Pacific Railway to being out on his own with three small children and a wife who left her career to raise them. I was a stay-at-home mom who did daycare to assist with finances. I can't tell you how often we ate Kraft dinner and Mr. Noodles!

At one point, we worked together for a period of seven years. It was great at the beginning as I was eager to learn and to please him with my administrative skills, and it was also challenging with our home life, as my kids went without parents in the home for 12-18 hours a day.

It came to the point where the two of us couldn't work together any longer; and our marriage started to suffer. My husband was able to come home after work and create a balanced work-life scenario for himself, but I on the other hand would never let work stay at work. It became apparent I either worked for him or stay married to him. I chose to stay married to my entrepreneur.

Times definitely got tough. We had cars repossessed, foreclosure on our home, our credit ratings tanked, just to name a few setbacks! But we persevered, ended one company, learned from it, and built our next company. If I could go back to the start of our journey and give myself advice, I would say the following:

Trust in yourself. You have a big role in the life of the entrepreneur, probably more than you give yourself credit for. The entrepreneur usually sees all things as a great idea, a new venture. They will promise the moon and the stars and nearly kill themselves unless you step up to the plate.

Learn when to set boundaries. They always have "whens"—when I finish this portion, when we have time to travel, when business is better – but few of the "whens" come into play as they are always onto the next bigger and better thing. Stick with them through the "whens" but make sure you trust in yourself and are strong enough to assist them and are aware of those times when you just have to say, "Whoa!"

Don't lose sight of the power of yourselves as a couple. There was a reason you married that crazy entrepreneur in the first place; make sure you both are the main focus and work in the "whens" around that.

Allow time for yourself. Don't get caught up in the entrepreneur's world and forget who you are as a person. Take time to follow your dreams and aspirations; it's not a one-way street. If you lose yourself in their world, you are no good to anyone, least of all yourself. Remember they married you for a reason as well, you balance out their crazy world!

Don't lose out to the business. Above all, make sure your key focus is always on each other. Don't allow the dream of becoming successful ruin the relationship you have with your spouse. Be willing to give it all up to stay together as a strong unit. Recognize that failure will happen but grow from each hiccup and move forward together as a team. Yes, he may run the business but without you being a supporting actor, the movie just isn't the same.

We now have a thriving business, and I know how to support and how to properly pull the reigns on my entrepreneurial husband to avoid conflict and to give him room to build his dream. He has taught me to be open to the universe and grateful for everything that comes into our world.

Chapter Four

Mind Your Team

> *"A chain is only as strong as its*
> *weakest link."*
> ~ ANCIENT PROVERB

Your Weakest Link Will Pull You Under

One day, while operating the skincare business, Colin and I had the shock of our lives.

I retrieved the company mail that day, which included a number of checks. I casually placed them on the counter before my husband.

Colin glanced down at the checks and said, "Who signed those?" I said, "You did." The color drained from Colin's face as he looked at me and said, "That's not my signature." I looked at the checks again and gasped, "Oh my God it's not. She didn't, she didn't."

We had hired a woman to work for us in an administrative capacity when we had the skincare business. She was a sister of a friend of ours and she'd earned our trust over time so we gave her more responsibility. Her position evolved to include managing the bookkeeping and accounting, although she didn't have a background in either. We didn't realize how complex it was, and we should have hired a professional—or at least someone whom we had properly vetted.

Colin can be a demanding person; he can unintentionally put fear into employees. This woman we hired wanted to please him so badly, that we discovered she would produce spreadsheets she knew would make him happy. She would show positive cash balances in the United States and in Canada, even when they weren't. Things looked rosy on paper. Not knowing she had put in fictitious numbers, Colin would react positively, "Oh wow! Excellent. Things are going great!"

Meanwhile, she was giving us a salary from a line of credit. If Colin had known that, he would have never taken it. She had been signing checks for the last *two years* we didn't know about. It never occurred to me to wonder why she always insisted that she get the mail for us. We thought, "Oh, isn't that nice, she's getting the mail for us." In fact, she was getting all the returned checks with her signature on them.

Up to that point, I hadn't been involved in the backend of the business. Now, it was clearly imperative I get involved. What else had she done that we didn't know about?

The next morning, our "bookkeeper" walked into work with coffee for everyone that the company had paid for.

Colin put the checks on the table and as she laid eyes on them, she turned pale. He said, "What else do I have to know?" She replied, "Your line of credit ..." and he said "Yes." She continued, "Well, you thought you'd only spent $70,000 of your $100,000 ... But, we have spent all of it. It's gone. There's nothing left."

We had thought we had $30,000 left to pay for an order that day, and our other overhead expenses. To discover we had nothing left was more hard-hitting than discovering the fraudulent checks from the bank. We had no safety net.

Nevertheless, I had to drive to Vancouver to pick up our order for $10,000 in skincare. As I was driving downtown crying, I felt angry, numb and confused. Before I left, Colin said, "Wow, we've been violated with our eyes wide open. She was right in front of us, and we did not see it. How blind can we be?"

I said to him, "Never again do we ever, over my dead body, give anyone access to bank accounts, credit cards or any of our money. No one will have a card on them. It's not going to happen." That was the day I unconsciously walked into the business without really being asked to. I thought, "You know what, this is my livelihood. If we got screwed, it was our own fault. Shame on me for allowing this to happen."

From then on, it became apparent how much damage had been done. We started getting our tax returns in from the United States. The California tax return stated,

"Please explain how you got to this amount." Colin said to me, "You handle this. You did accounting in 12th grade." I did—but that was back in South Africa, not America. With the commitment to not let anyone else into our financial matters fresh in my mind, I said, "Okay. Let's see what I can do." For those of you who are not aware of California taxes, it has to be one of the most complicated exercises you will endure. Each and every county and area has its own tax percentage and they all need to be calculated individually!

I first said a quick prayer and then called up the California tax office. I was blessed that day as I got the most amazing representative on the phone and after a 45-minute conversation, he had walked me through how to do a tax return step by step. On a side note, I did such a great job, they ended up owing us money!

Then I did the taxes for the other states in which the company was operating. On a recommendation from our accountant, we hired a qualified and experienced bookkeeper to clean up our books. She began teaching me how to take over the books. Because our previous employee hadn't had any bookkeeping experience, our books were a mess, but this woman taught me enough to get a basic grasp on things.

When we fired our office assistant, a forensic accountant said, "You know, you can sue her for fraud for at least $300,000." I said, "It would cost us $100,000 to sue her. We don't have the cash to sue her right now." My fighting nature wanted to sue her, but we chose not to go that route. Colin correctly advised, "Just let it go." We could have spent not only a lot of money but energy in that process; it could have been two years of chasing negativity with more negativity. Instead of chasing her, Colin said, "Calm down, it's okay, karma will get her."

So, we let it go. We've paid back our dues to the people we owed. There were some companies that closed their doors on us, but that's a part of doing business. Sometimes you have to override your emotions with what is best for you—and the business—in the long term.

Trust, But Verify

Once I entered the team as bookkeeper, I never left the company. As Make Your Mark has evolved from a mom and pop shop to a significant sized company, my role too has shifted, with our evolving accounting needs. About three years ago, we hired a qualified accountant and cash flow expert to work alongside me. The first words she said to me were, "I don't want access to your bank accounts. Don't ask me to pay a bill for you, don't ask me to pay a Visa." I replied, "I like you already."

We've learned whatever our weakest link is in the business, that's eventually what's going to pull us under. Even if you hire someone to deal with that weak link, you need to oversee everything that is going on in your business. You may not know the full ins and outs of that department but you need to at least know if that person is doing a good job. We had a Make Your Mark student once let me know he wouldn't be attending the *Winning Websites* course as he already had a website specialist. My response to him was that it's wonderful to hire an expert; however his specialist could be taking the wrong approach to the vision he had in mind. His need to not want to get involved could lead to a disaster. I advised him to take the course. I spoke from experience. At some point – as most entrepreneurs do – we made a quick and brash decision to hire an internal salesman for a 3-month contract. It turned out, his work ethic and style were so opposite to what our students were accustomed to that we quickly realized he wasn't a fit. Unfortunately we were left with doing some damage control and many apologies. Again another learning experience for us: when you are beginning to scale and put systems in place to replace yourself, make sure there is a match in core values.

Even though our bookkeeper is phenomenal, I will never let go of my role in the finances. She can see bank accounts, she can see credit cards; I can't hide anything from her. But she knows I'm watching like a hawk. She knows even if I go overseas on vacation, I'm monitoring the credit cards and bank accounts.

It took me a long time to find her, and I trust her. However, I like to say, "Never trust fully when it comes to your money. You always need to be in." It's not so much a matter of trust as it is responsibly managing your assets, or your business—which is what the business owner should be doing. That's where business owners often get screwed; some people don't want to see the money part. It scares them so they block it out and they let someone else take control. But you're giving a lot of power to someone dealing with finances, so you have to stay involved.

Your Strongest Links Will Build You Up

Gino Wickman, who wrote the book "Traction," has a philosophy of right person, right seat. In other words, place the most qualified individual for a position into that area of the business. When we don't follow this concept, we realize our mistake of putting a round peg into a square hole. Now, we only hire the strongest team members, "A" players who are the best at what they do.

At Make Your Mark we don't have departments, instead each area of the business is categorized as a "pod." We have a phenomenal "love pod," otherwise known as the client care team. This group of encouraging and heart-centered ladies are there to love and nurture our students. They are aware our minds can easily take us out of the game with negative talk and self-defeating statements. They have ability to assist our students with what we call the Universal Challenge Line or UCL. Let me explain what UCL is. When you run a race you only know what position you came in once you cross the finish line, but the biggest challenges arise often right at the very end, 100 meters before you cross that finish line. The same thing happens universally. Before you reach that desired goal, this imaginary challenge line comes up to test you to see if you are worthy of what is on the other side. Our "love pod" ladies understand the emotional roller coaster of an entrepreneur and on many occasions, have assisted our students into believing in themselves and the path they are on. On one occasion, our Love Pod leader personally delivered a student's binder and material to their front door as they couldn't come into the office. It's small gestures that speak volumes about the quality of your team.

Our longest standing team member, Cheryl who has been with us from the start, has graciously traveled around with Colin over the years missing out on many of her family's birthdays and one year, being away during one of her milestone wedding anniversary dates. We are so grateful to her for her dedication, passion and love for the business.

Make Your Mark would not be where it is today without these phenomenal and fierce team members, our strongest links, building us up.

Supporting the Team

We recently hosted a training event at our head office with students from across Canada in attendance. During lunch we went around the circle and each team member stated who they were and what pod they belonged to. When it came time for my turn, I said something I have never said before to my entire team. I described my role as a mother bear, who protects and looks after her cubs. Colin always uses the hashtag #MYMfamily and that is truly what we have built. My team know Colin and I are there for them always in any situation. A story comes to mind I'd like to share with you about this.

Our Love Pod leader was welcoming a new student into the program and was reviewing all the details about their new venture with us. Part way through the call he became rude and insulted her. She was taken aback but continued with the call in a professional manner. He, on the other hand, continued to be rude and so she ended the call. She came into my office in tears. After hearing the story, I decided to call him personally as no one has the right to be so rude to my team. In typical mother bear mode, I was protecting my cub. I made the call and we had a light-hearted pleasant conversation as we soon realized we had recently met the week before at our Business Mastery event. Once that was out of the way, I asked him why he was rude. He was asking us to change a policy for his own benefit and was upset the answer was no. Remember, when your clients change and dictate your rules and policies, they are in complete control of your business.

I have done a lot of personal development work and I immediately recognized him from the Hartman

Personality Profile (the main idea being all people possess one of four driving "core motives." The driving core motives are classified into four colors: Red, motivated by power; Blue, motivated by intimacy; White, motivated by peace; and Yellow, motivated by fun.) He was a Red type personality, typical of entrepreneurs and he was used to dishing out orders. I'm not a confrontational person; however, my thoughts were if you can dish them out, then you must be able take them too! After living with Colin for so long I have picked up challenging techniques along the way. My next few sentences were divinely guided as I informed him in no uncertain terms that he would not treat any of the MYM team members in that manner again. He was welcome to stay in the package as long he abided by our policies and should he choose not to, then he was welcome to leave. I had one stipulation should he choose to stay, and that was he would have to personally apologize to the woman for his actions and harsh words toward her. He humbly agreed to my offer and I handed the phone over to our Love Pod leader.

She later came into my office and gave me a hug. She had tears again; however this time it was for gratitude as she explained that never before had she experienced anything like that. She could not believe I had put her first and that I was willing to release a client in order to protect a team member. When you have amazing people on your team, you always put them first.

Marsha, a colleague of ours who is the COO of Legacies Health Centre Ltd, and her husband Matt know all about the vital role of having the right staffing in business. They have learned many lessons the hard way as well. It's times like these when having a support system is critical.

CASE STUDY:
Marsha Furlot, Legacies Health Centre

My greatest advice is: People will always tell you who they are. Listen the first time.

Our staff has been our greatest reward and challenge. Over the years, we've hired many wonderful and not so wonderful individuals based on having given everyone benefit of the doubt. Now we know to accept what our gut feeling says about a potential hire—and the results are much improved.

There are continuous highs and lows with owning a business such as staff problems, money issues and people dropping the ball. The good part about our business was having each other to depend on when things went south. Matt and I handle different aspects of the business but we are always on the same page about our common goal. In any department, when two sets of hands are needed to get the job done, we can count on each other, if no one else, to see it through.

Honesty and Humility

After the incident with the office assistant, we had to field those dreaded phone calls from creditors asking for money. It's amazing how in these situations the mind can go in so many different directions: Do I make up stories as to why I can't pay? Do I not take the call at all? Lots of negative talk definitely comes up, but ultimately we chose honesty and a whole lot of humility to speak with collectors. It was a difficult time for us and yet so many wonderful lessons were learned.

Now, when we receive calls from clients who tell us, "Listen, I can't pay you," we can empathize. We've been there. What we learned is we need to establish an honest and open relationship with clients. We communicate and encourage clients going through financial challenges to talk to us about it. Many a time my team and I will find an amicable solution to assist them. The worst thing they can do is keep quiet. If they're quiet, my mind wanders to, "They've run away, and they can't be trusted." Just be open with people. Say, "We can pay you this much. That's all that we can give you."

When we were in that situation we told the credit card company, to which at the time we owed $30,000, "We can give you $50 a month." If we owed a contractor or vendor, we would stay in communication with them. I used to report back every week, "I still don't have the money to pay you. The status hasn't changed." They appreciate the honesty—they just don't want you to disappear. And they want to know it is top of mind for you. When we came into money in the business pool, we paid them back. There was nothing more satisfying than clearing those debts even though it took a period of time.

If you're in a similar situation, it may require you scaling back your lifestyle some more. Everyone can be financially free as long as they live within their means. I've noticed in business groups there's a concern people won't hire you if you are not perceived as successful. It's hard to let people know that you are not paying yourself a salary, or you are in debt, or operating on a line of credit when you're talking to a room full of potential clients. You also may be uncomfortably aware you are being watched. This is the moment you need to put your pride in your pocket and remind yourself growing a business takes time, money and resources which don't always necessarily come to you at the right moment.

Being financially strapped is a lesson in humility. You may have to admit—to yourself and to others—you can't afford to eat out or have as many coffee dates anymore. Just be truthful. By being open and honest, you will feel better about yourself and this may help your creativity to flow, as it did for Colin. He was aware of how the change in lifestyle for him could have easily pulled him into a negative downward spiral, so to keep his spirits up during that time he started a reward system for himself. It's not that he couldn't buy himself a coffee anymore, it now became a reward for when he made a sale or actioned a difficult task on his to-do list. They were substantial actions and not trifle ones, such as I came to work today!

That experience has put Colin in a good position to coach others in Make Your Mark who are struggling with cash flow issues. Some people are young in their businesses, and they'll come in to explain their financial struggles and we'll tell them, "It's okay, that's normal." They breathe easier when they know it's just part of growing a business.

Chapter Five

Do Your Homework

"Diligence is the mother of good fortune."
~ MIGUEL DE CERVANTES

By 2015 Make Your Mark was well established in Canada. Colin had successfully built the company through all his networking efforts. That year, Colin went to a Mastermind group, where he met the most wonderful people, including Tom. Tom was a guy from Europe living in the States who came across as a successful businessman. He was a good talker, entrepreneurial, had a feisty spirit with a great personality.

Colin and Tom stayed in communication and Tom came to Canada to spend time with us on vacation. We had a great time all around. Tom was looking to move back to Europe. He loved what Make Your Mark was all about, and he wanted to start a Make Your Mark in Europe.

Instead of jumping the gun to have him start Make Your Mark in Europe, we thought let's crawl before we walk. Let's have him start a call center for us first—we called it a "Heart Center" because we don't like the term call center. He said, "No problem, I've got the right people. I've run call centers back in the States." So Tom moved back to Europe and ended up recruiting his dad, his brother, and his sister for the team, and they started the Heart Center.

Potential clients of ours would fill out questionnaires, and for the ones who didn't purchase, we'd send their questionnaires to the Heart Center for follow-up. These potential clients would then get calls from people in Europe, which led to a few sales, but it also made people angry.

Before long, we realized Tom and his team were big talkers. What they would tell our students was fictitious. Tom's dad was telling people he had mentored Colin personally and that he'd be at the events; he was claiming to be the go-getter behind the company.

We lost a few students because they didn't like the way they were talked to. We soon realized this call center was actually damaging us. When we said to Tom, "Listen it isn't working out how we want it to work out. Let's cut ties," he flipped a switch and said, "Fine, but we signed a contract and you agreed to pay this amount."

We signed a contract, but it was dependent on results which he wasn't giving us. In any case, we wanted to part on amicable terms. To do so, we ended up paying him about $30,000. He had threatened if we didn't pay him the full amount of the contract, he would go on social media and tell everyone we didn't stick to our word. He even said he did not care if we retaliated, because his name was already mud on the Internet and therefore we had way more to lose than he!

Colin vehemently protects our name and brand as it is not only us who can be tainted by negative publicity but also our team members and subcontractors. Unfortunately, even if they had nothing to do with what happened, they can get pulled in to it as well. No company wants a bad reputation on social media so, even though it basically became blackmail, we paid the guy.

Do Your Due Diligence

When we told a friend what happened with Tom, our friend said, "I knew he was a scam artist." I said, "Why didn't you tell us?!" He'd assumed we knew his background and were okay with it—that maybe we believed he was turning over a new leaf and we were giving him a second chance.

When we first met Tom, he said to Colin he had some businesses go sideways, and he wanted to change countries and get a fresh start. But he defended his background, and it got to a point where we felt maybe he was innocent in all the wrongdoings. When I Googled his name later, however, and saw his profile, I found out that, basically he had to leave the United States; if he didn't, there would have been someone coming after him.

He had scammed people out of millions of dollars. It really made us feel stupid, that we had fallen for his tricks. And it made us angry because he'd stayed in our house many times. Every time he'd come, he'd bring lavish gifts. He threw money around, even if he didn't have it; he lived the image that he had it, and he made you believe he was a good guy.

Now, any person that comes our way, we Google in advance and if I can't find anything, I ask myself, "Why can't I find a profile?" Recently, we wanted to hire someone in California to make follow-up calls to potential clients. My first words to my team members were, "Do you know who he is?" They'd say, "Oh, he comes through someone we know." I said, "I don't care who he comes through, do we know him personally? Can we Google him? Do we know his core values?" Tom had thrown us off track by charming us—we did not research his core values like we normally do.

For clarity's sake, core values are the fundamental beliefs of a person or organization. These are the beliefs that determine behaviour. Examples include: accountability, collaboration and trust. If we come across people who seem fantastic now, we stick to our system—how we interview, how we hire, and how we do our core values check. We've become much more cautious, which is another one of our life's lessons. That experience made us aware we must do our homework.

As long as you can learn from all these different experiences, and put them into practice every time, that's how you'll grow. If you keep making the same mistakes, then that's what Einstein calls the definition of insanity—doing the same thing over and over and expecting a different result.

So, with each experience, you're learning. Some lessons cost more than others—this was about a $50,000 learning lesson which in comparison, was substantially smaller than with the skin care company. Those losses are part of life. In our case, maybe we didn't learn completely from the bookkeeping experience. The way I see it is, if you don't learn from the first lesson, you get a second one to teach it to you again.

The "Gabi Test"

Tom may have pulled the wool over my eyes, but in general, I've developed keen gut instincts—to the point my gut has become an essential part of our company's "Profile Review System." It wasn't always heeded in the beginning, however.

At one point, we were looking to employ more people on the ground in a new area. A gentleman had been interviewed by Colin and another team member, and they seemed to enjoy him. I hadn't yet met him when I was flying to Toronto to go to an event he happened to be attending as well. As I landed, I got a text message from him—even just the text message got the hair on the back of my neck to stand up. Then I got to the venue and I met him, and within the first three minutes I knew, I just did not like this person. I couldn't tell you why, I just didn't like him.

In any case, that evening we went out for dinner and I'd never wanted to leave a restaurant so fast in my life. He just made my blood boil. Later that night I addressed the issue with the person who had hired him. I said, "I've got bad news for you, but I really do not like this guy." She was taken aback and said, "Well, we hired him, so let's see how it goes."

That man ended up costing the company many hours of frustration. He was terrible to deal with, by email or telephone. He couldn't get his facts straight. He got nothing in on time. It got to a point where a few clients were wanting to leave because of him. We had him on board for about 10 months before he finally got underneath Colin's skin. We realized he didn't have the same core values as the company.

At times we don't know why our gut instinct is screaming "No!" but we just know something isn't a good fit. Sometimes the answer is clear from the start, and other times it takes us a good 10 months. But it's all part of the learning process.

Over time (and many "I told you so" looks on my face) we've come to a point where Colin trusts my instincts more than anything. I have learned to trust the signs, symbols and synchronicities that come my way. He's learned, after 10 years, to listen to my gut instincts so much so we have recently installed a new office policy that before we hire anyone, he gets me to be in the interview. Candidates may have an impressive resume, however they have to pass the "Gabi Test" first.

Trusting your gut instinct can work in a positive way too. We were recently hiring for a new executive assistant for Colin and we had three candidates around the table doing a group interview. Within the first five minutes, my gut had picked who would be best-suited for our company and who Colin would relate to best on every level. I hadn't looked at their resumes and had no idea what their work experience was like. After they had left, we discussed each candidate and as our minds can and do, mine began to doubt the gut by what the candidates had said during question time. One of the ladies was the alpha in the group and so she come across as a good strong option and I felt myself leaning toward her. We reviewed their credentials and the one who I had picked initially had the best experience and was the most qualified for this position. I am learning more to always follow my instincts as they usually guide me on the right path. She has joined the MYM family and is doing beautifully – definitely the right choice was made.

I was recently told this statement and I am doing my best to always carry it out: "You need to listen to the small messages first, then and only then will the big message be sent to you."

Chapter Six

Trust

"Trust is earned when actions meet words."
~ CHRIS BUTLER

I've shared serious mistakes of ours along the way. With any of those mistakes, we could have given up. We could have quit the business, and I could have given up on my spouse. I believe, however, that hard times will always turn around, provided you put in the work and maintain a positive mindset.

One thing Colin has shown me is if you have a passion for what you do and you're dedicated, it can succeed. As long as it's a viable business—you can't just beat a dead horse. But your vision can come true, depending on your discipline in making it a reality. Many people give up too quickly. They hit one pebble in the road and immediately take themselves from the game. They offer up victim statements such as: The economy has changed. Bad things always happen to me. This is too hard!

There have been boulders in our way, not just pebbles. It's about how you overcome those hurdles—what mindset you have around them, and belief. Belief in the business—and belief in your partner. From the start, I told my husband, "I trust you to make it work." So, unless you can see a flaw in the business you can help them see, your role as a supporter is to cheer on your partner's ever-changing dreams.

With Colin being a visionary, almost every day he could come home with a brand new idea. As his supporter and cheerleader, I would offer an encouraging smile and just say, "Wow, great new idea!" Even with the skincare business, did I trust Colin it would work? Well, it was working. Then conditions changed. But I trusted in Colin if things went wrong, he had the drive and discipline to turn them around. If your spouse is wishy-washy and just wants to play business ... that's a different story.

I've learned over the years to trust my intuition and gut feelings. Sometimes they appear at the start of a venture before we even dip in our toes. And other times the feeling emerges when we have one and a half feet in. With the skincare company, even though it was a passion of mine to sell the product, I thought, "Don't do it, don't do it, don't do it." I'd been in the industry, and knew it was cut-throat. But Colin said, "It's going to be fantastic!" He was convinced it was the best thing to do at that time to enhance the business. My gut wasn't happy about it, but he went for it anyway. I sat back and let it unravel—I'd told him I would trust him, and I was afraid of crushing his dreams.

I recommend if you are an entrepreneur and your support partner's gut is saying, "Don't do that," find out why his or her gut feels as such. If you have a good gut instinct, then ideally get your entrepreneur to listen to you. It could save you millions. It could save you making a tough decision. Sometimes you can't stop your partner from making decisions but then—that may be where a tough lesson is learned to serve you later.

Trust Your Core Values

Colin's entrepreneurial drive started at a young age. When he was only 9 years old, Colin started working weekends at the local hardware store and later began his first business at 18. Even when he was an employee, he was always there to make sure profits were being made, and people didn't screw the company. His work ethic and intentions of success were there for the benefit and growth of the company. So when he said, "I'm going to go out on my own," it made sense to me. He had the drive, passion and the right attitude for it.

But if your spouse is someone who is not wired as such, his or her venture will likely not work. For those who lack business savvy, don't support their entrepreneurship—or at least send them for training or point them in the direction to get the right support they need.

Support comes in two different ways. There's before and there's during. If you sign up as supporter at the start of your spouse's business, be aware there's another level of support ahead.

It's one thing to verify core values of who you bring onto your team, but you also need to verify you have the same core values as your partner. It is less likely the business or your foundation as a support system is going to work if your core values aren't aligned. If your core value is family unity and your entrepreneurial spouse's core value is independence, there may be problems.

One of our students did a core value analysis with her husband, a firefighter. His core values were safety and security. He grew up in a household where there was no financial security, so for him those qualities are paramount. My client is a nurse, and she was comfortable financially with where they were at; she felt they could easily live on his income alone. However, she is working her job while she builds her business and writes her book, because they are clear on his core values. She hasn't quit her job to focus full-time on her business, even though she really could afford to.

Colin and I did a core value analysis for the family and for the company. Doing so will help with the growth of both. This practice will make the marriage stronger, as you both will be on the same path on how to run the family and interact with each other. Normally when couples fight, it's because someone has strayed from those core values. In business, a core values check plays a role in hiring new employees and even taking on suppliers.

As soon as you know your core values, quickly you can tell when someone is not in line with them. When you have that first conflict ask yourselves, "Okay, why are we clashing? Why are we being triggered by each other? What are our core values, and what is out of sync?"

Also, it's important you're not too vague with your core value words. Everyone says their core value is integrity, or authenticity. Find more meaningful words, because we should hope integrity and authenticity are understood as your core values. Having well-established core values is what will help keep you focused.

Trust the Process

When a partner decides to embark on starting a business, the first thought you might have is, "Wonderful! We're going to make loads of money as we are now self-employed, we can dictate our own paychecks and it's going to be great!" In reality, it can take anywhere from 24 hours to 10 years to see that dream come to fruition. Can you wait 10 years to get to this dream? You have to be prepared for the long haul.

In our case, with the pole dancing business the dream happened in the first six months. We thought, "Wow, this is pretty cool, this is so easy!" We then added skincare, which involved a whole new layer of investment, only to have our bubble deflated quickly when we got hit by the recession. With Make Your Mark, it may appear we had overnight success, but in reality, it has been more like a 10-year overnight success!

When things take a turn for the worse, that is the time to turn around negativity and ask your spouse, "How can I support you right now?" I have been down this road before, and I know this is no easy task—especially if you may be feeling like you have reached the end of your rope. Feelings of dissatisfaction, anxiety and stress may be where you are at. Promises of financial abundance, more time together and vacations are nowhere in sight. You may even hear yourself saying something like, "Ugh, it's taking so long." It's easy to forget saying so puts more pressure on the entrepreneur. It causes them to get pressure from both sides—from you, and from their own disappointment. That additional pressure will either cause them to work harder (not necessarily smarter), it could push them away, or it could lead to tension and fighting.

Trust the Timing

The majority of the human race lacks patience. To quote my mom, she always says, "There's only God's time." And it's true, we have no control over time. When the going gets tough, you need some kind of daily ritual to keep you grounded and to remind you, "It's going to happen when the time is right."

Looking back now at the timing of everything we experienced - the good, the bad and the ugly - it was all in the right time frame. If all events had unfolded and played out in a different sequence, we wouldn't have been able to deal with the situations. Out of every incident and experience we were subconsciously building a memory bank of lessons and solutions that would aid us through the next challenge and growth strategy.

Timing is always right, even when we may think, "Oh my God, really? How much more can I take? I'm at my end." It may seem like the end to you, but there's always a bigger plan ahead. I'm of the belief you're only given what you can deal with. I can look back at those hard times and say, "Wow, I actually got through that and I have the ability and capacity to endure change, risk and a lot of stress!" In a positive light, I also can see the strength I have gained.

Here's a story about how our clients, Rob Gallop and his wife Sarah, got through the initial tough years of Sarah's business, SGDI (Sarah Gallop Design Inc.).

CASE STUDY:
Rob Gallop , Sarah Gallop Design Inc.

As soon as my wife Sarah started her career as an interior designer, it was clear running her own firm was where she would end up. She has a passion, skill and entrepreneurial spirit that rivals most people I have ever seen. After four years of working in companies, she saw a better way and started SGDI out of the spare office in our townhouse.

I was making good money at an accounting firm. We had no children and a small mortgage, so we decided it was time for her to give it her best shot with a business of her own. Within six months, she had an employee and office space, and the team has slowly grown since. Being a CPA, I was involved from the start. I helped her with the books and invoicing on evenings and weekends to support Sarah and have the admin side of business not totally consume her.

It was probably a year into the business my permanent involvement became a recurring topic of conversation. Being Mr. Conservative, I was unwilling to commit so soon, as I would be leaving a very good paying job to help my wife in her design business, and therefore take a pay cut. Two years in, I bit the bullet and quit my job and came on part-time. Within four months, it was full-time.

As I am carrying the weight of the administrative side of the business and everything else that is not actually design, Sarah is able to focus on her strengths. She would be successful without my help, I have no doubt. But as her spouse I have unquestionable commitment to her and the business, something that would be impossible to find in an employee.

The fact I have a business and accounting background is a bonus that has helped us grow our design business into one of the most successful in Vancouver. Being in business together has strengthened our marriage immensely. There is nothing we cannot handle together personally, or in business. Many people think we are crazy for working together as husband and wife, but we could not imagine it any other way.

If I could go back to the start of our journey and give myself advice, I would say take a little more risk and follow your gut. Looking back, there were things we could have done years ago that we are doing now, that at the time seemed like crazy dreams impossible to achieve. We were much too conservative at the beginning (likely due to me, the accountant). Also, whenever something goes wrong in a relationship or situation, we can almost always track it back to a gut feeling we both have about something or someone. We used to ignore that feeling in the beginning, but now we are more in tune with our values and things that just don't sit right, and avoid bad situations.

The hardest part of our journey is now. We have had great success since the business started seven years ago, and very few problems or hiccups at all. We have grown a lot in the last two years and with that has come growing pains: Staffing problems, juggling of countless projects, managing more people and an unrelenting workload—work-life balance is not so balanced at the moment. We get through it by leaning on one another and discussing ways to improve and change how we run the business. Nothing can change overnight, but our goals are to balance work and life so we can enjoy business success, but not at the expense of our family or relationship. Being in it together has been invaluable.

The greatest lesson we've learned is we can overcome anything. As difficult as any situation could be, we are resilient and we are a strong team. Difficulties and struggles are seen as opportunities and we push each other out of dark places in our minds and motivate each other. Alone, it would be much harder.

Chapter Seven

Work-Life Balance

*"The key is not to prioritize what's on your
schedule, but to schedule your priorities."*
~ STEPHEN COVEY

Colin and I share the core value of quality time. When Colin walked away from the mining company to begin life as an entrepreneur, he did so thinking he would have more time to spend with the kids. He didn't have to travel as much with the new business—but he had underestimated other demands that characterize life as an entrepreneur.

In reality, being an entrepreneur means long hours packed away in an office in solitude. It requires being deliberate about making time for the family, and setting aside time for play. In our family, we make Sundays family day. In fact, we call them "Fundays." We didn't do it in the beginning—at first, Colin just worked all the time. But after a while we realized if we didn't set aside time for the family, it wouldn't happen. We needed a set of rules.

Set Office Hours

For entrepreneurs, there is no such thing as set, regular office hours! They work until the job is complete, sometimes doing an all-night stretch if needed. This only can be sustained to a point, however, before burnout sets in and productivity goes in reverse.

Here is a discipline that should be followed for your mental and physical wellbeing: You need to set office hours, even if you work from home. Put a sign on your door, maybe from 9 a.m. to 3 p.m., or 9 a.m. to 5 p.m. Once you have completed your set time, put up a different sign that says, "Office is now closed."

Set an alarm clock. It will help keep you sane, and also define your work schedule so your family knows not to interrupt you.

Having an office space in a commercial building has assisted both of us in establishing normal working hours. When we ran Make Your Mark from our basement, our offices used to be in our guest rooms. The commute to work was wonderful, but as convenient as it was, I had to train myself to not work all the time.

Before adopting rules, I was burnt out and tired, and I discovered I was less productive than when I took time off. There is a large body of research that is clear: working harder does not make you more productive. In fact, the opposite is true. In a study of consultants by Erin Reid, a professor at Boston University's Questrom School of Business, managers could not tell the difference between employees who worked 80 hours a week and those that didn't. And even an entrepreneur who is working long hours voluntarily (or out of necessity), is more likely to make mistakes when tired. Overwork and the resulting stress can lead to a variety of health problems including poor sleep, depression, impaired memory, and heart disease. Keep overworking, and you'll progressively work more stupidly on tasks that are increasingly meaningless. In short, take time off. I understand now there will always be work to do but working weekends does not actually get me ahead, it just makes me crankier and our family time suffers.

Pssst...You're Not an Employee

Colin has had to remind me, "You know, there's no rush to get to the office." I had always sought to start work at the same time in the morning as our team members. I have to be reminded I can go in at 11 a.m. now if I want—and I don't have to feel guilty about it. I needed to shift my mindset into that of an owner, not an employee. I had always seen myself as an employee until Colin said to me, "If you were to divorce me, you'd become an owner very quickly. You would realize half this business is yours." I was like, "Oh." It didn't even cross my mind half of it is mine.

I've promoted myself from employee to owner and moved out of the employee mentality. This has allowed me more freedom from the business and time to take a day off here and there with Colin for no other reason than because we can!

Take Vacations

Our family didn't take a vacation for three years—partly because we couldn't afford to. We finally got an opportunity to go away and upon our return made two discoveries. First: We both micromanage. While we were gone, the company ran smoothly without us! Second: When we got back, we were 10 times more productive.

A vacation doesn't have to be an exorbitant undertaking. You can just take off the weekend from turning on your computer. My Fridays are everyone else's Fridays now, too. Colin still often works on weekends; he's a workaholic just like me. When he's working my mind goes to, "Well if he's working, then I might as well work too," which is a bad trap to fall into. For the past three years, however, we have been fortunate enough to take off at least three months of the year in total. Even when our schedule is jam-packed with back-to-back events, what keeps us going is knowing we have time off booked.

I always wanted to have only a three-day work week. For years, Colin has been saying to me, "That's totally doable." It's only now, after I spent a lot of time away this year, that I've learned it is doable. I can easily take off Fridays, and another day. We've grown so much we're at a point where my team can take care of things. They don't need me right this minute anymore. I used to think, "I've got to get on this right now!" But really, I don't.

I realized I was bottle-necking the business because I was trying to do everything, and had my hands in everything. Now I take the approach of, "Get this along to the next person, so I can focus on what I'm really good at." It's hard to let go of what I used to do, but I have to give some things up in order to get ahead.

Everything comes back to remembering priorities—which may be setting time aside for your family, time for yourself, or time for the couple—before you get into bad habits. Bad habits will attempt to creep in, I promise you. You'll get the work bug. In my case, the house could be on fire, and I would still be working saying, "Hang on, I'm not done yet."

I've probably missed out on many good private times I could have had with my kids. There are many times I could have brought out the puzzle when they were smaller, instead of sitting there working. Can I get that back? No, I can't. I know, I'm guilty.

Colin would say when you first begin, you have to put in the hours. There can't be any days off when you first start. There's no one to say, "Sure, I'll do it for you. Go sit on the beach all day." But there does come a point when you have the maturity in your business to know what you can and can't get away with.

We once had a student who was in the startup phase of her business. She wanted to make about $10,000 a month; however she also wanted to take an hour-long bike ride at lunch time and end work at 4 p.m. This is a wonderful work-life balance once you have established your business and are generating the desired income. Needless to say, she wasn't a diehard entrepreneur and has subsequently gone back to working for someone else.

Set Rituals

Once you set a ritual, sticking to it is the next challenge. It's easy to have a goal, and it's easy to break it. It's like planning to go to the gym today, and then today becomes tomorrow, and so on. Sticking to a routine can be difficult. A trick could be giving yourself a reward when you manage to stick with your plan.

Colin and I go to a particular local restaurant every Saturday afternoon. It's our way of getting out. If we don't leave the house and do something, we're going to sit at home and work. We crave that time now. It's become part of our ritual and it's put into our schedule.

On Sundays, we have ice cream with the kids and we go to the gym. What is the ritual you want to set? Maybe it's going to see a movie every Friday night. Commit to scheduling something—anything—to break you away from work.

How to Manage Both Spouses Working from Home

Recently, I've been away on courses so Colin and I have been like ships passing in the night. Often, when I return home he leaves for somewhere else, and we might not see each other for two weeks. The positive outcome to this situation is when we see each other, we have a lot of new and exciting conversation.

When Colin worked with the mining company, he'd be gone for two days or 2-3 weeks at a time. He'd come home and the conversation would be fresh, and it would be great to see each other again. Then when he started Make Your Mark, he'd be home 24/7. I found myself thinking, "Don't you have somewhere to be? Can I pack your bags and send you somewhere? You're really crowding my space." It took time for me to get used to having him home.

Then, with the expansion of the business across Canada, he had to begin traveling again. It's been a roller coaster of transitions. At first, I was saddened by the thought of him leaving and I found myself missing him since I was now used to him being at home. The more he began to travel, however, the easier it was for me to adjust to him being gone. Now, we share a hug and kiss goodbye, and life carries on.

I cherish our time together, as it is so sporadic. I've found a vacation to be a good bonding time. Lately, with Colin's schedule and the additional expansion of the company, we haven't come home from vacations together. He flies off somewhere for business, and I come home with the girls. It takes a willingness to maintain the relationship and bond even though we're now apart much of the time.

We have found time apart keeps the marriage solid. It works well to take breaks. Some months my team will come in and say, "Just so you know, you won't see Colin much." I take it in stride, knowing we have booked those vacations. We plan our trips appropriately. We know we have a reward coming up, and that's what keeps both of us going.

I believe that's what creates a successful marriage for entrepreneur couples: Time away from the business, where you can just enjoy being together.

Ron Comeau is a client of ours whose wife Elaine is founder and CEO of Easy Daysies, a company that produces magnetic visual schedules for kids and adults with memory loss. She also owns a chapter of "Mompreneurs Canada," while Ron helps to run the family photography business. With three kids aged 8 to 13, it makes for full days. Here is their story.

CASE STUDY:
Ron Comeau, Easy Daysies

Elaine was an elementary school teacher prior to starting her own business. She had little entrepreneurial experience, but she has the "DNA" of an entrepreneur, and has always been unstoppable. Elaine's company was launched two days after our youngest child was born, if that's any indication of how fierce and committed she is. Soon after, the company started garnering media attention and grew faster than we had envisioned. A few years later, we appeared on the pitch show, *Dragons' Den*, and from then on, there was no looking back.

While I do accompany my wife to trade shows and help with website and product design, I'm not a paid employee. My direct involvement with the business is limited. What I am is a "sounding board" for my wife to share her ideas, thoughts and strategies, and she considers me a valuable partner in decision making.

We are often taught to "hope for the best, plan for the worst." If I could go back to the start of our journey, the advice I would give myself would be: plan for the best! Given that Easy Daysies took off fairly early, I would have treated the business as though it was a bigger deal, hiring experts to take it to the next level earlier than we did. For example, I could have hired a bookkeeper instead of doing the books myself. This would have left more time to increase marketing and product development.

The greatest lesson I have learned from being in business with my wife is the trials and tribulations faced together inevitably make us stronger as a couple. When we do a trade show or business deal together, we have a shared common experience. Launching ourselves into what many people would call marital suicide has brought us closer together, as has our Christian faith – I would highly recommend a big dose of faith (of any kind) to any couple considering this journey.

In marriage, there will always be conflict. It's the same with business partners. When spouses volunteer to be both, you open yourself up to more chances for conflict every day. It is said women are more likely to blend all aspects of life together (spaghetti), while men like to compartmentalize different aspects (waffles). I can relate to that as a man. I like to compartmentalize work and home, and being "partners in business, partners in life" is not the easiest way to do that. Throughout our entrepreneurial journey, we have learned how to navigate our way through conversations in a way that works for both of us.

I understand what it is like to be an entrepreneur— to have the responsibility of a business growing or dying in your hands. My advice to others in the position to support an entrepreneur is to notice and learn (preferably by doing) what it is like to be the sole life support for something – a business, a baby, a pet, a plant – then apply what you have learned to supporting your spouse. Would you tell an infant's mother caring for her baby that it is a waste of time? Instead ask if there is any way you can help. The same applies to supporting our loved ones in business. Now more than ever society needs to support more entrepreneurs who bring brilliant ideas to the table, in the execution of these ideas. Yes, we need bosses and employees, but we need brave, creative people who will work today to invent tomorrow, and we need to support them all the way.

Chapter Eight

Communication

> *"Communication is a skill that you can learn.*
> *It's like riding a bicycle or typing. If you're*
> *willing to work at it, you can rapidly improve*
> *the quality of every part of your life."*
> ~ BRIAN TRACY

Don't Crush the Dream

I've made mistakes as a support person for my husband.
One thing I've found that has really crushed him is when
he comes to me with this "great idea" and he expects me
to say, "Wow! That's great!" and instead I say, "Seriously?" Sometimes my responses back to him haven't been
what he has wanted to hear, and he gets thrown off. It's as
if he were a kid coming to me with a brand new toy and
I tell him, "Your toy sucks."

I've crushed a number of his dreams without realizing
what my actions were doing. I could have done so with
just a facial expression or a simple word or a lack of interest or understanding of his idea. Now, my best tool is to

listen and absorb his idea and then ask questions, and to keep my face more neutral.

*D*on't be too quick to criticize, rather than compliment your partner. Don't be too critical, without knowing all the details. We forget entrepreneurs are like artists. They're creative; they have an idea in their mind but they might not even know the full picture yet.

Remember they are coming to you with their first step—it's a vision, but it's not necessarily a fully formed business plan. They cannot show you anything concrete yet.

A good example of when I learned to not be too judgmental too quickly is when Colin said he was going to hire a marketing guy from the United States to help us. Prior to that, we had hired quite a few consultants within our different businesses. We paid them well and got very little for what was produced, so unfortunately our track record with consultants—particularly those from the United States—was not looking good. So when he said he was going to be hiring Jerry, I was quick to pass my look of distrust and say, "Seriously? Another one?"

But I'm glad to say that Jerry panned out to be the real deal. He's phenomenal. I should have held back on that, "Seriously?" and not have been so quick to jump down Colin's throat. To me, all I saw were dollar signs going out the window. Sometimes you just need to see what happens. The proof is in the pudding.

Plant Seeds, Not Forests

Colin has wanted to expand to the United States many a time. I've really held back those reins and bit my tongue, or I'll slip in an, "It's not the right time." I'll even tell my accountant to tell Colin it isn't the right time. I've felt until we were solid and income was flowing freely—when we had money packed away and everything was 100 percent a well-oiled, systematized machine—we weren't ready to expand. I remember Oprah once saying if you expand too quickly, it can kill you. It's like putting your finger into more pies when the first pie hasn't baked yet.

I've therefore been Colin's dream crusher by saying, "Not now." I had watched as we went to the United States when we started the pole company; the minute he put his focus there, the business in Canada started to go down. When you take yourself away from the business' primary focus, things begin to drop. Until the business can run without you, don't change your focal point.

But here's the trick—instead of being a dream crusher, make your partner think your idea is their idea. Otherwise, your spouse probably doesn't want to hear it. Many a time I've said things Colin doesn't like hearing. After he takes time to process it, he often comes back and says, "Hmm. Dare I say she was right." But what I've learned to do is plant seeds, instead of trying to put a whole tree in front of him. If I put the whole forest in front, he gets upset because now I'm interfering with his dream.

Instead of telling your spouse what to do, say, "Have you thought about doing it this way?" Then I'll hear him say my idea back to me, believing he came up with it. When it comes from your entrepreneur's mouth, it's way better. Normally, entrepreneur personality types like to be right. I may not get the credit for my ideas, but I'm not there to get the glory. If it's going to help others, that's what I care about. It's not my stage.

Check the Ego

If you interviewed the wives of some of the top businessmen, the sad part is quite a few of them would be divorced because many of those men were too volatile to live with. The ego often kicks in too much. One thing Colin said to me from the beginning was, "Please keep me in check. If my ego goes up, kick me in the ass." I said I would gladly carry out that wish if needed.

When we first started the business, I would have been too scared to say, "Honey, you're getting a big head." My fear was mostly about how he would respond to a comment like that. It is said with age comes wisdom, so my approach now would be more like, "Colin, that's not you." Or I'll ask him, "Does that fit your core values?"

Effectively communicating with your entrepreneur is an art form in itself. Timing is everything. If he or she is in a mood or is distracted, it's the wrong time to even attempt a discussion. I've learned how to talk to Colin—what to say and when to say it—and that's made all the difference.

Everything Comes Down to Love

To be a good supporter you need to be prepared to ride the wave through the ups and downs and trials and failures and be by your spouse's side, loving him or her. I have trust in Colin that he'll provide for the family in every way. Even if the business were to fail, I would still love him. Everything comes down to love. If there's love in the household, it can hold you together. People say it's the strongest currency, and it is.

No marriage is perfect, but we are blessed to have a good marriage. Our communication is getting stronger. I don't hold back in fear of saying wrong things. The other day I said to Colin, "I just want you to know that going forward, there might come a time when you say let's go do something and I don't want to and I'll say I don't want to. Just so you know, be prepared." He's used to me normally saying yes to everything, even if I don't want to do it.

I've not been subservient, but codependent in the past. And it isn't a conscious thing, it's just a habit that developed from our culture. I grew up in a chauvinistic South African society, where women have been socially controlled by what men say. Even if this status is not taught directly to you, it's what society dictates. My mom worked for my dad, and not by choice. It was dictated to her, and so it was demonstrated to me that you work for your partner. I didn't know anything different.

With the personal growth courses I have been attending and the wisdom I have gained over the past few decades, I'm now at a point where I say, "Hmm, I don't want to go to this place. I want to go somewhere else." I need to be truthful to me. I discovered I co-depend. Co-depending is not speaking or living one's truth for fear of upsetting, angering, disappointing or hurting the feelings of another. I've had many opportunities, however, to practice letting go of that fear.

Know When to Speak Up

When Make Your Mark only had the three of us in the company, I was juggling different hats every day. I was mum. I was wife. I was bookkeeper. I was receptionist. I could feel how it was getting to a point where I couldn't handle all the juggling.

Make Your Mark was a new business. It was building slowly; cash flow was not the way we wanted it to be. With any new business, there is a stress factor. During the day, I worked at a table next to Colin. There were days when he would get stressed, and I would be the person who he would take it out on. You always take out your frustrations on the one you love the most, so there were times when that got stressful for me.

I remember one day I took my children to school, and I was driving home. I'd never felt so down. I had this deep pit in my stomach, and I was convinced I had to go out and get a job. I felt I had to make money to contribute to the family, in order to relieve some of the stress. I came home, and I was at my end. I'd never been so fearful, as well as brave, in the same moment.

I sat down next to Colin and said, "I've got to talk to you. I either work for you, or I am your wife, but I cannot do both anymore. I cannot wear all these hats anymore. It is draining me. I cannot be the punching bag during the day when things go wrong, and then have to be the loving wife at night." I sat there with my heart in my throat, and finished, "Either I work for you, or I'm married to you, but I cannot do both anymore." As soon as I was done, it felt like the weight of the world had been taken off my shoulders. I felt pride in myself to have said what was bugging me.

The first thing Colin said was, "But, you don't work for me, you work with me." I replied, "Well, honestly, I feel like an employee the way that you tell me what to do and boss me around, and I cannot take it anymore."

He was quite taken aback by that. He wasn't expecting it from me, because I'd always been a reserved, quiet person. I was calm during the whole discussion, but I opened up and shared how I was feeling. I wasn't leaving him,

I just couldn't do both anymore. I couldn't juggle. I was mentally at my end.

Colin walked away to go think about what I'd said. He came back having realized he needed to be cognizant of the way he spoke to me during the day when we were working together. I think that conversation was a turning point in how Colin viewed my strength. He learned not to undermine me as simply a follower.

In our case, that situation had a happy ending because of our strong marriage and good communication. We knew we were soulmates on this journey. Without that foundation, it could easily have broken us. From there onward, we communicated how we were feeling with each other during the day. We also realized we need to take breaks—from each other, and from work.

Challenges like this will come up if you work with your spouse or partner. It's fine, in a way, to be able to speak your truth—to stand in your power and say what you mean in a way that makes you feel understood and respected. There are times for exercising that right, and there also are times when it feels right to let it go—or as I like to say, to put on your Teflon suit.

Put on Your Teflon Suit

Just as my children know even if I shout at them I always love them, in our marriage, Colin and I know we can take out our frustrations on each other but always love each other. Sometimes Colin gets upset about something in the business that isn't perfect, and I'll be the one who hears about it. But his growth has come to the point that if we are short one handout at an event or such, he realizes it's okay, we can fix it. He's learning it isn't always going to be perfect, and also things happen for a reason.

However, sometimes he'll slip back into old habits, and he'll question me on something that doesn't really apply to me—something a team member may have done. In that case, I have to just let it roll off my back, to remember he's just letting out his frustrations. Now, I pull out my union card and say, "It's not my job. Go talk to them." That's the best thing about where we are with our business right now—I can just say, "It's not my department." If you want to talk finance, come talk to me. If you want to talk about any other area of the business, go talk to that department, or "pod" as we call them. What I have realized is there are times he just needs to vent in a safe, loving environment.

He knows I'll put on my little Teflon suit and say, "Come, crack at me. Dump it all. Okay, you're done? Great let's move on." He can now download all his frustrations on me without me taking it personally. Entrepreneurs need to de-stress somewhere, and you cannot always go to the source. If he spoke to the team the way he spoke to me, they wouldn't be with us anymore; they would have said, "Buddy, I'm out of here."

But that took years of practice for me to not take things personally. I also learned when emotion is high, intelligence is low. Conversely, when emotion is low, intelligence is high. When I'm emotional, I might say something to Colin which would hit his emotions and bring down his intelligence. There's a snowball effect, so you can either be a supporter, or you can be someone who drags down another person.

This whole journey has given me the strength to find my voice, to speak up, and to encourage myself to be more diplomatic. Colin is a strong character. If I were married to someone else who didn't have his dominant character, I might have been a different person.

Colin has changed a lot through the business as well. What would have made him snap back when we started the business now makes him say, "It's okay." I'm like, "Wow! What happened?" So, he's grown, which has helped our marriage as well. He believes in what he teaches – when you grow personally, your life and business grow exponentially.

Support for the Support

People feed off each other's energies. If you're stressed out and then you're holding your spouse's feet to the fire saying, "You promised X, Y, and Z," or a certain dollar amount in the bank account, then they get that fear energy as well. That negativity pulls your partner down even further.

As a supporter, there are times when you need an outlet for your frustrations, too. When you are not feeling positive, speak to other entrepreneurial spouses and say, "Hey, listen, we're going through this challenge, do you have any suggestions?" Most often, all people need is someone to just listen to them. They need to talk themselves through what's bothering them and then they feel better. We aren't always looking for advice. We're looking for someone to speak to who is in the same boat, so we can believe we're not alone.

During the pole dance business days, three times a week after I dropped off my girls at school, I would walk with two other moms for 45 minutes. This often would become my support group/counseling session without even realizing we were doing this. Karen was supporting her husband in their successful business and Sue was an accountant who was self-employed. Looking back now at the synchronicity of having those women in my life, it couldn't have come at a better time. Karen's husband at the time owned 16 retail stores and each year he would open another one, so her knowledge and experience of being the support role was invaluable because it gave me an insight of my journey and an understanding of this new lifestyle I had taken on. Sue, on the other hand, would offer valuable accounting advice and would always clarify my questions and concerns. It was a win-win in many ways as I was feeding my body with exercise and my mind with reassuring thoughts.

Don't take it all by yourself, because there are many people out there who have been through what you're going through. Even the other day, a friend called me—she's the entrepreneur, her husband is not—and she's bending because he's not supporting her, and all she wants is his support. I reminded her he grew up in a household where everyone had jobs, so that's all he knows. If she needs support, she has to go out and find it.

Even as a little girl, I have always adopted the attitude everything will always turn out right. Unfortunately, we are human, so doubt has a way of creeping in to test our strength and beliefs. Even with all the challenging experiences that have come our way in business, with people scamming us, things have always turned out okay in the end. We always land on our feet. Since I know we'll be okay, that is what I project onto Colin.

If you have a pessimist for a support person, it can be detrimental. If you need support you aren't getting from your spouse, have a venting session with someone else. One of Colin's favorite analogies is, "If you want to better your game in tennis, then you need to play an opponent who is stronger in the game than you." The same applies to getting ahead in life and business. If you want worthwhile support from those who have been through what you're going through, then seek them out and ask them how they got through it. Offer to treat a millionaire to lunch and pick his or her brain. You will be amazed by what you discover.

Take a look around you at who is in your circle of influence. Who do you ask advice from? Who do you hang out with? Are these people raising you up or putting you down? Take your observations even further, to include what outside influences are around you. What kind of music do you listen to? What television shows or movies do you watch? The actions you take because of these influences all play a huge role in your success.

In the past 20 years, our circle of friends has morphed substantially. It began with wonderful people who were like us, working a job and living an employee life. Today our circle is made up of entrepreneurs who are all driven to achieve success in their business and family lives. What is beautiful about the latter is we all encourage each other and celebrate each other's wins along the way.

Chapter Nine

Working Together

> *"Teamwork is the ability to work together toward a common vision. The ability to direct individual accomplishments toward organizational objectives. It is the fuel that allows common people to attain uncommon results."*
> ~ ANDREW CARNEGIE

I've been approached many a time by men who enthusiastically say to me they'd love for their wives to work with them. My first response back to them is, "Make sure your wife wants to work with you in business. Don't assume she wants to. Ask her, don't tell her."

It was never my lifelong dream to grow up and work with my husband in his business. In my mind, it was his design and his brainchild and I was there to contribute. Then again, my role model was my mom working with my dad, so it felt normal when I was brought into the business.

From an external point of view, it may look great for husbands to work with their wives. But there's an impact behind the scenes. If you've just started a business and it's just the two of you, each will pretty much be in every department. As your business grows, you can departmentalize and not be on top of each other, but until then it can be a rocky road, and boundaries need to be set.

Don't Always Talk Shop

Before I got involved in our business, conversations with Colin revolved around what had happened in his day of business activities, and what had happened in my daily activities with our girls. But as soon as I got involved in the business, almost every meal we had out could have been a business expense because we always talked shop.

Even on vacation we talk shop, because it's all we know. If we don't talk business we feel like, "What do we have to talk about?" We talk about the girls, but then when that's done what do we have left to say? Somehow we always get back around to work, because it's a common theme with us. We even made a game around "no shop talk after 6 p.m." The rules were simple: The first person to mention work had to pay the other one $5. Day one, at 6:03 p.m. I broke the rule. On day two at 6:15 p.m., Colin was so excited to tell me something that happened that day my $5 came back to me. And so the week continued. We never got past 6:30 p.m. and the money just kept changing hands. Eventually one of our daughters told us to give it up!

We are equally responsible for that habit. When you are with an entrepreneur who is passionate about what he or she does, it's hard not to discuss that passion. The same goes for me—of which Colin has found a loving way to remind me.

Create Sacred Space

It's only once I officially came into the company with the spa business that I got the true sense of what a sleepless night was. Until then, I slept beautifully. Colin was the one who would roll around, tossing and turning, worrying about money and people suing us, and I was none the wiser. But as soon as I came into the business and realized where we were financially, I would stay awake in bed thinking about how to pay this bill or pay that one. I never thought I'd ever be in that position. Thoughts which I never had before, these foreign dreams and nightmares, were now mine, and unfortunately I was in them.

One pet peeve Colin had about me being in the business was that I don't know when to stop talking business. My biggest downfall is that, like him, I am a workaholic. So, I would climb into bed and say, "Do you know that this client didn't pay us, and that client didn't pay us?"

Finally, Colin said, "Seriously, do you have to bring accounts receivable to bed? I'm trying to get lucky here. I don't want to talk about accounts, unless it's a transaction to my accounts payable. Can I be the account receiving right now?" It totally broke the tension. I realized the bedroom is our sacred space. No business, no stress, no tension. The only transaction should be between him and me.

I did a healing session a few years ago. She said I had to find a way to physically disconnect from the business at night. She recommended before coming to bed, I picture all of my attachments to the business falling away. I had to cut the cord, so to speak. Every night I therefore picture myself cutting the cords of work. I tell myself, "I don't need to know if someone will pay me today or tomorrow. It's not important right now. Now, I need to disconnect."

Colin can disconnect fairly well. He can compartmentalize. He can decide to go on a diet and be on a diet right that minute—he doesn't need to plan. He can go, "Okay. Business is done. Let's lock the door." To me, I carry it with me all the time; I don't know how to turn off. But I can tell you without that off button, it will burn you out. And your marriage will burn out.

Breathing New Life into Marriage

Since Colin and I are often together all day long, feelings aren't necessarily shared after work. Essentially, the marriage and work gels into one. There becomes no distinction in our day, so there's no distinction in our communication either.

What is beautiful is the exploration of self, or when each of us doing our own thing, leads to fresh, new communication. This generates new interest in the partner. There will be a new emotional connection with each other. By taking a personal growth course, for example, there is a breath of fresh air coming into our conversation. It causes us to dig deeper into the emotions of each other.

There is a statement Colin always says from the stage, that I've told him I disagree with. He says, "Working together will never improve your marriage, it will keep it the same or make it worse." He loves that statement, but I feel our marriage is stronger because of working together. We have gotten to know each other in all different situations. I know his pressure points, and I know how to read him.

If we both did our own jobs, I wouldn't know his character so well. I've learned how to communicate with him. Working together doesn't strengthen your marriage by itself, but it has helped me to get to know him deeper and more intimately in a whole different sense. It's true, if we look at when we first met, he did his job and I did mine. I didn't know how he behaved at work, or who he was there.

When we first got together, before we even came to Canada, he came home one day and started telling me what to do. I turned around and I said, "I'm not your secretary." It's a side of him I didn't know, because I didn't know him at work. To me, I feel it's strengthened us because I have learned who he is in all environments.

129

Here is a story shared by one of our clients, Jessica Kerkhoff, about what she learned was necessary as the support system for her husband, John Kerkhoff, and his business Mr. Build Contracting Ltd. Chilliwack B.C., New Construction and Renovations.

CASE STUDY:
Jessica Kerkhoff

As the wife of a successful entrepreneur, the best advice I could have given myself at the start of our journey would be to continually connect with my husband—whether it be date nights, mini-holidays, or week-long vacations. As I am always busy with children and him with growing the business, I find it is important to have frequent meetings of the hearts.

My greatest lesson learned throughout the last 22 years is to have patience. Patience because paychecks arrive randomly, not on a specific schedule. Patience because my husband is a busy man. Patience until we get to spend time with the kids before they go to bed. Patience until we can focus on each other for a little while. Yes, patience practiced is patience learned.

Chapter Ten

Mindset

*"We are responsible for what we are, and
whatever we wish ourselves to be, we have the
power to make ourselves."*
~ SWAMI VIVEKANANDA

Dream Boards

Colin has always been big into dream boards. A dream
board can be as simple as a poster board with images cut
from magazines, quotes, or photos that represent where
you want to be. You need to hang them on the wall in a
strategic area where it is seen daily to remind you of what
you are striving for. With the amount of time we spend
on a computer daily, some people even have them as their
screensavers so when their open screen times out, their
dreams appear front and center. But here's the thing—after you make the dream board, then you actually have to
do something toward those goals.

Yes, you could meditate, you could do visualizations,
you could use gratitude journals, but you also have to do

the work. A dream, for example, could be wanting to go away on a dream vacation with your partner or family on a cruise ship as a reward for exceeding your annual targets. You'd be surprised, however, how the simple act of creating a dream board can lead to practices that build momentum toward your goals.

At the end of every year, it has become a family tradition to review our boards and check off all the accomplishments that have been achieved. We then create new ones with our next set of goals and dreams. It's always mind blowing to realize how much of the desired events, material possessions and vacations have come to fruition.

Destiny Profiles

One practice that evolved from this manifestation work was our decision to meet with a Feng Shui consultant. She then turned me on to the "Four Pillars Destiny Profiles." These are personal profiles built on science that tell your future. They aren't like using a magic ball, or having a tarot card reading, but rather they use birth data to forecast your year ahead, according to Chinese science. If you complete a profile at the beginning of the year, it will tell you whether it is going to be a good year to make money, or a good year to hire new people or to take a year to study. When you know what's coming, you can create the best strategy that will facilitate you in your goals.

Humans all go through cycles. There are one-year cycles and 10-year ones. Almost everyone goes through a challenging financial and relationship cycle. If you want to open up a business and your profile tenured you at the start of a 10-year bad cycle, then maybe it's not the best time. Knowing your destiny could help you to avoid beating your head against the wall, wondering why nothing is working. Your profile would clearly tell you it isn't the time to be doing what you're doing right now.

Now, you might have a profile done regularly and discover it seems it's never the right time to start your own business. To this, the consultant would say, "Start the business, but just be prepared that it's going to be a harder journey to do it this year than in a different year." Ultimately, don't let a destiny profile keep you from your dream—just consider it a possible tool to help you start off on the right foot.

Our consultant might tell Colin after reading our profiles, "This year you're going to have challenges in your staff." One time she even told us, "Some of your team members might move on this year." She can even tell us exactly who we might have issues with. I must admit, she's been spot on; she's pinpointed things about us and our business. We might think some of the things she's predicted are preventable, but they're not. However, having a bit of a bird's-eye view of what's going to happen that year helps us better prepare.

Destiny profiles also have helped me better understand who Colin is. In Colin's profile, he's Yang Fire which is the sun. He is the eternal optimist. He will always rise—he will come out tomorrow, and the day after that, and the day after that. So with him I know, it doesn't matter where he goes, whatever he puts his finger on, there is going to be optimism behind it. He sees the good in everything, and I have learned that's his character. My profile is Yang Metal and metal needs heat and fire which come from the sun. My profile also showed I have an internal struggle when it comes to my family and working, as both take a strong preference in my life – hence my previous statements of being a workaholic and dedicating myself too much to the business instead of my children. There are a number of different aspects that a profile is made up of and I'm not going to go into them all. What I know from our consultant is that Colin and my profiles are compatible on many levels and so our connection as a couple is solid.

By knowing his optimistic profile, Colin might say things like, "I'm going to invest in 10 different projects." I'm like, "*Ten* different projects?!" My mind is going, "Oh my god, he's literally going to invest in 10 different projects right now," whereas in his mind he means, "I'm going to research these projects first, get to know who I'm working with, and I realize not all of them will go through." I've learned, therefore, his optimism doesn't replace his business sense.

Enneagrams

Another avenue Colin and I have explored to better understand each other are Enneagrams. An Enneagram, if you're not familiar with it, is a model of the human psyche. The Enneagram can be seen as a set of nine distinct personality types, with each number on the Enneagram denoting one type. It is common to find a little of yourself in all nine types, although one of them should stand out as being closest to who you are. This is your basic personality type.

I'm an Enneagram 9, which is a Peacekeeper, and Colin is an 8, which is a Challenger. The Peacekeeper is receptive, reassuring, and complacent and resigned, whereas the Challenger is self-confident, decisive, willful and confrontational. (These are merely highlights and do not represent the full spectrum of each type.)

We are opposite in personality types, so we complement each other perfectly. We don't fight or raise our voices to each other, and though we don't always agree on everything, we know when and how to approach a situation in order to maintain a calm and happy environment.

If I'd have known all of these facets of Colin before we started this whole journey together, it could have been a smoother emotional ride. Admittedly over the years, I have figured out through trial and error a number of Colin's personality traits on my own. Now, with conclusive evidence it was reassuring to hear it from experts that I had read him correctly. Otherwise, some spouses might have packed their bags and left after discovering a particular facet. Instead, they can understand it could even be a quality that, if not there, also would mean the quality they fell in love with in their partner wouldn't be there, either.

Gratitude

Visualization, meditation or keeping a gratitude journal can be just as important as making the sales call. When people get in a scarcity mindset around, "I need to make money," the first thing they should do is gratitude and meditation. When I get busy, my self-care naturally goes out the window. I've had to learn to be protective of that time, and not feel guilty about taking it.

After I do gratitude and meditation, I'm in a different head space. I've had the time to reflect and be grateful for what I have. Instead of thinking, "Crap, there's no money," I'm thinking, "Thank you for what we do have. Thank you for the roof over my head. I am grateful that I'm alive this morning. I am grateful that I can move my arms and my legs and I can breathe."

If you're in a position where you don't know where you are going to find your next dollar, you may be thinking, "Yeah I can breathe, but I need to feed my kids." Those thoughts will still be there, and the emotion as well. But remembering what you have shifts the energy around it.

So, find your happy place; use self-talk to calm yourself down, so you can focus on what needs to be done right now. All of that worry is just going to bring you more worry, and worry attracts the opposite of what you want. The Anglo-Saxon definition of worry is to choke, so as we worry, we stop the flow of energy. When dealing with clients who are going through challenges, I always offer them the analogy of water flowing through a garden hose. As long as there are no buckles or kinks in the hose, the water will flow. Our worry and negative mindset is what causes those kinks and prevents opportunities from flowing.

At our core, we are human and I, too, have a tendency to fall back into a worry state from time to time. There are still times now that I think, "We're doing very well right now, but what about tomorrow?" I don't think that ever stops. But with awareness, the level of worry can be lowered.

It's important to remember the universe is not on our timeline. I know any abundance I'm experiencing today is the result of mindset work I did probably a month ago. If I'm in scarcity right now, it might not show up today or tomorrow but rather next month or the next. So, if you do your gratitude and meditation today, it doesn't mean that tomorrow things will change. You need to consistently maintain that raised vibration. Stick with it—it will come back to you.

It Happens for You, Not to You

There is a well-known statement that things don't happen to you, they happen *for* you. I always felt I was just helping Colin with the business and needing to support him—that I was not living my own dream, but rather living his. But the more I remember things don't happen to you, they happen for you, I begin to realize maybe this whole role of supporting him is leading me to unleash my spark, my desires, my dreams—which I've put on hold for years.

My role to this point has been to be in the background. Not to play small, but to be behind-the-scenes supporting him, and taking it all in. Through this journey, I've been discovering aspects of what I want to do and what I don't. I've watched how the ego can come in and take you over.

I've had to go on this journey with Colin for my own personal growth. It's not just about his growth and the business's growth, it's about my growth, too. So, when you have a partner who's going to be an entrepreneur, think about this:

> *What is your purpose on this journey? Why have you been chosen to be the support role? Is there something you need to learn from that role? Are you there to teach your spouse something?*

There's always a lesson behind everything that happens in life. Those lessons don't always show themselves on day one. It might take 10 years before you find out the lessons. But, if you are there supporting your partner, you are there for a reason.

Keeping the Faith

During the downturns, it's important to keep the faith that things will turn around—otherwise not only your business, but your marriage will be at stake. You need to dig deeper during those times and say, "I need to get back to why I married you. Why did we get together in the first place?" Remember that you can survive difficult financial times, you just need to live within your means. It might mean changing your lifestyle, so you are not going out to dinners as frequently, or downsizing your home to a more affordable mortgage.

You can make it work, if you are prepared to step outside of the box. Don't let money be your controlling factor. Yes, you have to eat, but at times you need to think about how you can do things without money. What can we do to be happy and get back to the roots of our love? Love won't feed your hunger, but it will feed your soul.

Suffering is a choice. It's a choice to feel like you are being dealt a bad hand. Or, it's a choice to say, "How do we fix this? How do we think outside the box?" There were times I wanted to say to Colin, "Just go get a job!" But that wasn't really the answer. The answer was to keep the faith, and to envision things changing.

Before bed, Colin and I used to read an excerpt from Esther and Jerry Hicks' book, *"Money and the Law of Attraction."* This became a daily ritual for us; some days we were 100% focused on it and other times we were just doing it out of habit. Every time, though, by the end of reading it we felt up-lifted and more positive about our situation. It was so well-read the page had become dog-eared. For the full excerpt, refer to the original work, but here is a shortened version:

> I like the idea that money is as available as the air I breathe. I like the idea of breathing in and breathing out more money. It's fun to imagine a lot of money flowing to me. I can see how my feeling about money affects the money that comes to me. I am happy to understand that with practice I can control my attitude about money or about anything. I notice that the more I tell my story of abundance, the better I feel.
>
> I like knowing that I am the creator of my own reality, and that the money that flows into my experience is directly related to my thoughts. I like knowing that I can adjust the amount of money that I receive by adjusting my thoughts.
>
> Now that I understand the formula for creating, now that I understand that I do get the essence of what I think about, and most important, now that I under-stand that I can tell by the way I'm feeling whether I'm focused upon money or lack of money, I feel confident that in time I will align my thoughts with abundance-and money will flow powerfully into my experience.
>
> [...] It is very nice to know that my only work is to align my own thoughts about money with my own

desires about money, and that whenever I'm feeling good, I've found that alignment.

I like knowing that it's alright for me to occasionally feel negative emotion regarding money. But it is my intention to quickly direct my thoughts in better-feeling directions, because it's logical to me that thoughts that feel good when I think them will bring positive results.

I understand that money will not necessarily manifest instantly in my experience with the changing of my thinking, but I do expect to see steady improvement as a result of my deliberate effort to think better-feeling thoughts. The first evidence of my alignment with money will be my improved feeling, my improved mood, my improved attitude-and then real changes in my financial situation will be soon to follow. I'm certain about that.

I am aware of the absolute correlation between what I've been thinking and feeling about money, and what is actually happening in my life experience. I can see the evidence of the LOA's absolute and unerring response to my thought, and I look forward to more evidence in response to my improved thoughts.

I can feel a powerful leveraging of Energy in being more deliberate about my thoughts. I believe that at many levels I've always known this, and it feels good to return to my core beliefs about my power and value and worthiness.

I am living a very abundant life, and it feels so good to realize that whatever this life experience causes me

WHAT THE... I DID NOT SIGN UP FOR THIS!

to desire-I can achieve that. I love knowing that I am unlimited.

I feel tremendous relief in recognizing that I do not have to wait for money or things to materialize before I can feel better. And I now understand that when I do feel better, the things and experiences and money that I want must come.

As easily as air flows in and out of my being-so it is with money. My desire draws it in, and my ease of thought lets it flow out. In and out. In and out. Ever flowing. Always easy. Whatever I desire, whenever I desire, as much as I desire-in and out."

Sometimes it's Okay to "Splurge"

Although I said you may have to adapt your lifestyle to accommodate challenging financial times, there can be an exception to this rule. As the spouse, you need to have the mindset required to support the entrepreneur, and therefore you need to do what it takes for yourself to remain in a space of positivity.

I've been in a situation where I wanted a pedicure, although I knew I should spend that money on more necessary things. A pedicure is $40—not a whole lot of money, but in terms of what that pedicure could offer me, it's priceless. It's going to make me feel luxurious. Or, it will make me feel the abundance I need to feel right now, so I can be in the mind space to support my spouse better.

142

Or, it will give me the confidence needed to close a deal. Something that may seem frivolous, isn't always.

Colin once booked a short trip for us in a nice hotel room. I thought, "We can't afford this," but he insisted, "We're going to go away. We're going to get a nice room." He knew being in a space that creates positive, abundant energy, causes you to produce more of it. It's not about opulence—there is a balance, but it is important.

Here's a tip: When you feel like you shouldn't do it, you should do it. Go out for lunch one day to a nice place, somewhere new. Sit in the sun and feel like a queen and see if it doesn't pick you up. When times get tough, check in with yourself, "Hey, am I going negative or am I still in the positive zone?" If you're dropping into that negative zone, your partner will pick up on it.

As the support system, strive to keep your mindset in a positive, abundant place — which is easier said than done.

But, when you're dipping into your pennies going, "It should be a gold mine," a change in mindset is like turning coal into diamonds. It takes years to change, but find a way to pick yourself up, because otherwise it will indirectly affect the entrepreneur and your relationship. And, it is only with high pressure that coal ever turns into diamonds!

143

Holistic Way of Doing Business

Colin has never been a fan of the "corporate business world" and so we have made a conscious decision to evolve Make Your Mark into a holistic business. Instead of thinking outside the box, we have removed the box altogether. By doing so, we have created a culture where our team members all have positive mindsets and beliefs about the company and their roles within it. We have no management per se, only leaders. Everyone is empowered to follow their dreams and aspirations. We continually celebrate wins no matter the size and always begin our day with an intention. This happens at our daily "thrive meetings" which are no longer than 15-20 minutes in length. Here the team is updated on what's going on for the day as to our live events and we go around the room so each person can share what they will be working on for the day. This way, there's no need to ask people afterward what their priorities are as we have just announced them and it creates a clear and united team.

Being an entrepreneurial company, we have come to realize some of our team members will move on at some point to start their own businesses. Even though it breaks our hearts to see them go, we are OK with this as we love the fact they feel inspired enough to start on their own.

We hire and fire according to our core values and not just a resume. Core values form a solid core of who you are, what you believe, and who you are and want to be going forward. They define what your organization believes and how you want your organization resonating with and appealing to employees and the world. Core values should be so integrated with your employees and their belief systems and actions that clients, customers and vendors see the values in action. They are the practices we use every day in everything we do.

This type of business strategy is considered by many experts to be fundamental to achieving the desired success. To reach the right goals, a proper foundation must be laid. These are the core values of Make Your Mark and the meaning behind each one:

COMMUNITY OF TRUST
Knowing we are doing the right things for one another all the time.

RESPECT THE INDIVIDUAL
Respect people and their property for the individuals that they are.

UNCONDITIONAL GRATITUDE
Giving gratitude in all situations, even if you have not benefited directly.

COMMITMENT TO EXCELLENCE
Never compromising on quality and always striving to improve in every way!

OPEN TO POSSIBILITIES
Always looking for solutions within the boundaries of the company.

INTEGRITY
Doing the right things, at the right time, all the time!

When a new team member joins the MYM family, they are welcomed in a warm and loving way. They get their own personal plaque with their Feng Shui destiny profile, their DiSC® profile results and Sacred Gifts on it. We also put on the plaque what style of communication the new team member would like, such as face-to-face or written. This serves as a guide for everyone in the office because at any time we can view these plaques and understand how each person operates. These plaques hang on the wall in our Brilliance Room, which is our reference to the board room. The word "Brilliance room" has a better energy to it and we have painted our core values on the walls so they are displayed and we are constantly reminded to live by them. We have a very open policy with all our team that anyone can call someone out should they be out of alignment with the values. We also have each person fill in a dream board which sits next to their personal plaque. Colin's passion is to assist our team in achieving their goals and so whenever a person's anniversary date comes due in the company, we will look at their boards first before we get them a gift. Obviously, some dreams are a lot larger and so we find appropriate gifts pertaining to that dream.

Many people believe how they operate and run their personal lives is different from how they should operate their professional lives. From my experience, they are one and the same. How we build and nurture relationships with friends is no different than how we should build and nurture relationships with clients.

The same goes for handling our financial affairs. If you can't balance your personal books and spend within your means, there is scant hope you are going to be any more aware of your habits when it comes to spending and planning for the business. One affects the other—if you wish to see more abundance in your business, you can start by nurturing your relationships and your finances at home.

Colin is a firm believer of the motto 'work hard, play hard'. For those of you who know Colin, this next activity won't surprise you at all. Friday afternoons between 4-5 p.m., we dedicate that hour to wine time and chilling. It's amazing how much you can learn about your team in a fun and relaxed environment. We have learned the value of taking off time to recharge your batteries and so we recently said every team member at Make Your Mark gets five weeks leave from the day they start. This allows them the luxury of taking long weekends and even doing overseas trips. It's a definite win-win as our team gets more vacation to unwind and then return fresh and ready to take on the world, and the company gets a more productive team.

Chapter Eleven

Look How Far We've Come

"Even when you think you have your life all mapped out, things happen that shape your destiny in ways you might never have imagined."
~ DEEPAK CHOPRA

With Make Your Mark now, we don't owe anyone money. We've paid back all our debts and are self-sufficient. We didn't like having the burden of owing people; it just didn't sit well with us. It is through Make Your Mark we were able to pay back debts from previous companies.

After having been through all those learning experiences in each and every business, we are now so much better equipped and prepared for the future. We have numerous "life policies" in place and are making sure our children are set up for success. We have a cash flow predictor for the next three years out and are continuously striving to better our systems and processes.

I can't give the best business advice, but I can give some. I have learned so much from this whole journey in every aspect, whether it's business or personal, mental or emotional mindset. If you step into a role as a support person thinking, "What's in it for me?" I can tell you that, if you're open to it, there is a lot there for you. I always thought, "Oh, I'm just there to support my spouse." I didn't realize, subconsciously, how much I'm taking in as well, how much I am learning through the process.

It may be my spouse's experience I think I'm riding on, but I'm really right there with him, having my own. It never dawned on me before, but now that I'm looking inward, I realize, "Wow. I've had an experience of a lifetime on this journey." It's something I never dreamt I would ever do.

If you just allow yourself to be open, you'll be amazed at what you will get out of your journey. Good and bad, because even your worst experiences are giving life experience. It's about how you receive them, and how you use those lessons.

At times it may not have been what I "signed up for", but I know I was meant to take this path. I was meant to be on this journey. I was not meant to be the driver - my role as co-driver was more important this time. Realize there is a bigger picture for you too, you might not see it at first, but there is. Don't spend time trying to find it, because it will find you.

Even with all our different accomplishments, I'd never taken the time to step back and take it all in. I've just taken things in stride. Last year's Christmas party was the first time in our 13 years as entrepreneurs I sat back and said, "Oh, my God. Look what we've done!"

We have over 20 people on our team of whom we are responsible for their livelihood. We are responsible for helping them pay their mortgages, car payments, and other costs of living. It hit me, "We have so much responsibility, but look at what we're creating!" I came home from that Christmas party with tears of pride and the thought, "Oh, my God. We've done it."

The company wasn't just the two of us anymore. It's Colin and me, and a beautiful family we have nurtured and raised. It took me a while to get that what we created is real. We had seen our friends and other people do it, but now we have done it.

In January of 2017 on a quick vacation to South Africa, I was talking to my dad about our business and the role I have in it. While I was excitedly explaining how we operate, I saw a side to my father I have never seen before, except perhaps for the day I got married. I saw pride in his eyes. He showed a respect for me on a whole new level. Here was his little girl, who was a beauty therapist, and a mom, and a wife sharing with her father how far she had come and how much she had grown.

It was the same with Colin's parents. His dad was always telling him, "Get educated, get a job, and get a career." I don't think they believed he could make it as an entrepreneur. It has been one of our proudest moments to show our parents, "Look how far we've come."

The People We've Met, The Places We've Been

As entrepreneurs, we've been exposed to people in all different areas of business, personal growth, and spirituality. With Make Your Mark we've come into contact with people like Jack Canfield (the co-author of "Chicken Soup for the Soul" books), Marci Shimoff (who wrote "Happy for No Reason"), motivational speaker Marcia Wieder, and John Gray (author of "Men Are from Mars, Women Are from Venus.") Colin has met and spent time with Sir Richard Branson on his island in the British Virgin Isles. He co-hosted a charity event with Evander Holyfield and smoked cigars with Arnold Schwarzenegger. So many doors have been opened for us, and so many amazing people have come into our lives.

What I've discovered after meeting these celebrity entrepreneurs is they're just people. They're people like you and me. They've maybe had a lucky break or they've made their own luck in life. They've succeeded, but they have been through their own trials and tribulations, and their paths of no money. They all had a ride somewhere on the rollercoaster. Some might have had a greater loss than others, some might have had a greater gain, but they all had to begin somewhere. Imagine what the roller coaster ride must have been like being married to Walt Disney. He had to experience going bankrupt seven times before finally hitting the jackpot! I'm sure his wife never signed up for that.

I never thought I'd do so much in my life, and the business would lead to so much. With the pole dancing company, we gained notoriety in the public and the media in Canada and internationally. We traveled to different countries launching the business. Colin and I appeared on television in South Africa.

In the United States, we even were featured on Judge Judy—someone took one of our business owners to court. The client had booked a party, paid the mandatory nonrefundable deposit and then canceled last minute! Our Pole Lot of Fun business owner had two wins that day – she won the case and gained a huge amount of new business. To top that off, we got invited to Los Angeles to attend a function at the Playboy Mansion. The theme was Mardi Gras and the Playboy Bunnies were wearing nothing but painted on bathing suits and a jillion beads around their necks. What an amazing experience that was. For all the men there, I have no doubt it was a fantasy come true!

We've been able to travel more than I could have imagined. The growth of the business has given us the freedom and financial reward to enjoy different parts of the world locally and internationally. It also has allowed us to bring our families to Canada for vacations so grandparents and grandchildren can be together. In June 2017, we celebrated our 20th wedding anniversary and Colin went all out for it. We didn't have the means to celebrate all the previous milestones because of raising our girls and building businesses and experiencing life's challenging lessons. But now we are making up for it and Colin and I went on the most amazing 8-day adventure to Bordeaux, France. We stayed in beautiful French castles, drank wine in old cellars with some of the world's most renowned wine makers. We dined with our own personal chef and were driven around with our own personal chauffer. We even slept in a billionaire's bed, soaking up all that billionaire energy... yes, please!

What an amazing reward we both deserve from all those years of sacrifice.

The ride was worth it.

Chapter Twelve

Time for Me

*"It's not selfish to love yourself, take care of
yourself, and to make your happiness a priority.
It's necessary."*
~ MANDY HALE

E specially in the earlier days of entrepreneurship, it
was tough to manage spouse, kids, and business. People would tell us, "Wow, you've really got it together!"
I wasn't so sure we did; the piece missing was me. I didn't
have *me* together. I was so busy supporting everyone else
I forgot to support myself.

I didn't give myself time for internal struggle. Perhaps
it was necessary at the time; how could I have been of any
support and strength to my spouse, if I was crumbling
and weak inside? My needs were a small sacrifice for the
bigger picture.

Starting in 2016, I began going on personal growth courses, which is something I continue doing just for me. It's caus-
ing me to think more about myself—what triggers me and

why, what has happened in my past and with my parents that could be affecting me today. This reflection is helping me understand why things are happening in my life.

My goal is to start finding more girlfriends. I had a realization when I moved to Canada that I put a wall around me to protect myself and didn't realize I was lonely. For the past 20 years, I had no support structure of my own, so I became the support structure. I buried myself in the business as a way of keeping busy so I didn't feel lonely. I subconsciously chose not to get close to girlfriends because of a fear of losing them again.

By moving half way across the world from South Africa to Canada, I left behind everything I had, and I felt like there was a loss in my life. I've always held back, just in case I needed to run. Even once we settled in Canada, I've known we could always end up moving tomorrow. I didn't want to get attached to anything again that I'd have to say goodbye to. I've kept myself in a close safety net all these years. But it's time to let go of those fears; I need to, for my own growth. I need to have an external support system and friends I can talk with besides Colin and my daughters—who are teenagers now, and don't need me as much.

My New Journey

I remember in December 2016, I had a tough time because I realized my kids didn't need me as much, so I felt pushed aside by them. Then Colin said to me, "By June next year, I want you out of the business." And I thought, "Great, that's two for two. My girls are pushing me away, now he's pushing me away." I felt rejected, thinking, "But I've been here for you guys! Come on, you can't just dump me now."

I cried. For those who know me, prior to doing my personal growth course, I wasn't someone who cried. There's a steel block that keeps all my shit together, but I cried. I thought, "Why am I crying?" It threw me, and then I realized, "Wow! I'm being kicked out of the nest." The little birds have grown up and they're kicking out mum, never mind kicking out the babies. But really, it's a beautiful thing.

Colin wasn't dumping me, he just needs me in a different way now. He doesn't need me to run the day to day things with him; he doesn't need me to be there as his cheerleader. I don't need to say, "You can do it!" because we've done it. Now we're onto what's next. We've hit the glass ceiling; the company is out of my depth now.

There's a parallel between having a company from the start and having kids from the start. My kids are older now and need me less, but I'm there to support, love and nurture my kids. In terms of the company, it is at a point where I'm there to love and nurture Colin and support him, but it's at a whole different level now.

There's pride in knowing we've raised the business like we've raised our girls, and we're getting to the point with both where I am starting to have more freedom. This freedom, in turn, has made me realize the lessons I've learned along the way as well as given me a vision for what's next for me. The growing independence of the business and our children is what's allowing space for me to step into the forefront, to start to live my own passion and dreams.

With each and every business there has been a different aspect of me growing. With the pole dancing company, I came back to life; I reawakened the old Gabi. I felt more feminine and confident, which served me well with Make Your Mark. Now, I can see how it gave me strength in a different way—strength to stand in my power, strength to speak my mind and speak my truth, strength to follow my gut.

Now that Colin and the kids don't need my support as much, I'm finding I have the time, energy and desire to support others. I've always been the light to illuminate Collin's path so he can do what he does. Now I want to simply point that light in another direction—to illuminate the pathway for other women, in particular.

When Colin pulled me up on stage last year and made me talk about this book, I thought "Okay, Colin this is my worst nightmare come true right now because I don't like public speaking." But I thought, "Crap, I'm here, I better do it. Let's get it together, girl." And I did it. I came down off there thinking, "Wow, I'm proud of me."

Since then, I've had the realization that I *want* to be up on stage speaking to people. Someone said to me recently, "If I could have had all of this knowledge at 21, how great would that have been?" Then she said to me, "Why don't you teach others on this path, so that they can be better prepared for the journey ahead?" I became excited about that idea. I could see myself on stage as a guide to other women. This book is the beginning of that new journey.

The Not-So-Silent Partner

Looking back at my childhood and the role models I had, I can see why I chose to take on a support role. My mother stood behind my father while he built the business. She was "the wife of…" and "the mother of…" The time has now come for me to no longer be "Colin's wife" or "Ruby and Jade's mom" – it's time to reclaim Gabi and stand in my power!

I initially considered titling this book, "The Silent Partner," because one of the greatest lessons I've learned on this journey is that silent doesn't mean weak. In fact, I believe it sometimes takes greater strength to stand strong behind the scenes, than to stand on stage.

There comes a time, however, when the silent partner needs to speak up. The best way to describe this transition is to picture a beautiful peacock with its feathers all down. Bit by bit as one grows internally, he or she comes face to face with childhood anger, fears and disappointments. By releasing those fears and emotions one by one, the beautiful feathers begin to open up and display the beauty that was hidden there all along, for everyone to see. Although I may not have signed up for this journey when I married Colin, I wouldn't have it any other way.

Another one of my mother's memorable phrases I refer to on a regular basis is that your life is a book filled with many chapters. Every person comes into it for a set reason. Some may appear in a sentence or two and some may be continuous throughout a few chapters. Regardless of length, they are all there to teach us something from an experience, to an emotion of life's greatest lessons. I am grateful to every person who has appeared in my book of life as they have all contributed to who I am today.

You've read about my journey, but this book is really about helping you to live your journey. If you are a supporter who needs support—that's what Colin and I are here for. There are so many of us "supporting roles" out there who have been through or are going through the same challenges. You are not alone. Reach out to us at **www.MYMsuccess.com**. We'd love for you to come on a journey with us.

To your success!

Additional Resources for Your Success

As you by now understand, if you didn't already—no one achieves great success alone.

Learn more about how you and your entrepreneurial spouse or partner can apply the contents in this book: Attend the event, *Business Mastery — Power in YOU!*

These are the key ingredients you will learn at the event:

- Powerful words that destroy you, your success, and your relationships.
- How to think like the wealthy and drive your personal and professional results to extreme levels of success. Eighty percent of success comes from the inner game of psychology, and twenty percent comes from skill and knowledge.
- Why knowledge and skill are not the keys to success.

- Why your own mind is often your worst enemy.
- How to train yourself for natural and automatic success.
- How to break through your invisible sales and income barriers.
- The cause of virtually all financial problems and all financial success.

If you've bought this book or received it as a gift, you can attend this event for FREE!

If you received this book as a gift from a Make Your Mark student, you may see a Success Number entered in the box to the right. Please use the Success Number when confirming your complementary attendance for the *Business Mastery — Power in YOU!* three-day event. Full details for the Business Mastery event can be found under LIVE EVENTS on the **www.MYMsuccess.com** website or by calling our office toll free (North America) at **(+1) 844-560-5609.**

Congratulations for taking the first steps to finding out the key ingredients that separate the millionaires from the strugglers! By doing so I would like to award you a certificate to attend our "Business Mastery – Power in YOU!" Program

Valued at $2,996

To register and for more information go to

www.MYMSuccess.com

or call Toll free (North America) at
(+1) 844-560-5609

Use Success Number: _____
When you register

(If there is not a Success Number above,
quote CPID335)

*This offer is limited to the Business Master – Power in YOU! seminar only, and your registration in this seminar is subject to availability of space and/or changes to program schedule. This is a limited time offer and the course must be completed by the date shown on the website. The value of the free admission for you and a companion is $2,996 as of June 2017. You are required to give a credit card number to secure your booking. A no-show fee of $100 will be charged for less than thirty-day cancellation. Participants are responsible for their travel and other costs related to attending the event. Participants are under no obligation whatsoever to Make Your Mark or Gabi Sprake. Make Your Mark reserves the right to refuse admission.

OTHER RESOURCES FROM
COLIN AND GABI SPRAKE
AND MAKE YOUR MARK

Make Your Mark offers a specialized process and system of experiential courses and groups in all areas of personal growth and business to maximize the results in your life and business. All events are designed to help students learn, apply, and develop the key ingredients in the Entrepreneur Success Recipe to become hugely successful entrepreneurs, which means making significant money and having maximum time off.

Here is a list of the courses and groups that are part of the dynamic SUCCESS SYSTEMS we designed to help you achieve maximum results and abundance.

Visit **www.MYMSuccess.com** to sign up or learn more.

BUSINESS SUCCESS SYSTEM: Seminars

BUSINESS ESSENTIALS

BUSINESS SHERPA™
ESSENTIALS
SUCCESS SYSTEM

Business Mastery—Power in YOU! (three days)

This seminar will transform your financial future forever. You will learn how to win the money game both in life and business, and achieve outrageous levels of success to live the lifestyle you want!

Business Plan 101 (one day)

A business with a set of crystal-clear core values and a written plan achieves massive results. This course takes you through a detailed plan of generating a one-page business plan for your business! Vital for all business owners and entrepreneurs.

Exposure Warrior (one day)

Get your business out into the marketplace quickly and effectively with unbelievable results. You'll learn key growth strategies that will have your business growing more quickly than you ever believed possible.

Sales Warrior (two days)

Two days of learning the opening and closing techniques to make more sales than you ever have. Double your sales in sixty to ninety days with true heart connection!

Marketing Warrior (two days)

Create marketing materials that WOW your prospect and turn them into paying customers! Learn an entire step-by-step process you can use for the rest of your life and in any business!

BUSINESS BRILLIANCE

BUSINESS SHERPA™ BRILLIANCE SUCCESS SYSTEM

Profit Warrior (one day)

Learn how to manage your money like a multimillion-dollar business. Understand how and when to find money long before you need it! By the end, you will be in complete control of your business.

Winning Websites 1: Maximizing Traffic (one day)

A website without traffic is like having a salesperson who does not sell! You will understand how to get onto the first page of Google and dramatically improve the traffic to your site.

Business Excellence (three days)

This annual event has six guest business experts who will walk you through multiple areas of your business to maximize profit, minimize taxes, and protect you and your business.

Hire/Fire 101

The biggest liability after your mindset are the people you hire to assist you in your business. There are critical items you need to have in place to ensure you hire the right people and keep them. This course takes you through everything you need to know around hiring, firing, and working with subcontractors to the maximum benefit of your business.

BUSINESS ELITE

BUSINESS SHERPA™ ELITE SUCCESS SYSTEM

Exceptional Customer Service (one day)

Turn your customers into raving fans by giving them a memorable experience every time they buy from you. This is the quickest way to growing your client base and income.

Winning Websites 2: Converting Traffic (one day)

Once you have turned on the traffic faucet, you need to be able to convert it into leads and money for your business.

You will learn the key connection strategies to maximizing conversion of prospects into clients online.

Social Media Wizard (two days)

This course teaches you how to utilize your time more effectively by turning your social media activities into lead generation and income. There are three secrets to a solid social media system that will be shared to turn your activities into income.

Own Your Greatness (three days)

These three days will take your experience at Business Mastery—Power in YOU! to an entirely new level of manifesting the results you want on a daily basis and achieving significant levels of financial success and time off!

GROUPS

BEST Mindset Groups

Business education is an essential part of a growing business, especially during the start-up phase. These groups meet every two weeks to set goals, hold you accountable, and assist with business education, tools, understanding and discussing challenges, and keeping your sales pipeline full. These are absolutely essential for entrepreneurs and business owners without staff and/or in start-up phase.

KAP-IT Success Groups

Meeting monthly as your own personal board of advisors, these groups are comprised of 5–7 established business owners who want to go to the next level of success. It's all about business owners assisting business owners with life and business experiences to ensure you save tens of thousands of dollars and maintain balance between work and life. There is an application process to belong to a KAP-IT Success Group, because you have to be focused on results and have set items in place and be willing to be held extremely accountable.

Legacy Groups

Colin lives by the statement, "Build a dynasty, leave a legacy." Only two of these groups will ever exist and have ten highly successful businesses in them. Quarterly retreats are held for four days with business experts, life coaches, and personal mentors of Colin to assist business owners to put in place all the structures and systems for succession planning and truly leaving a legacy. Membership is by application only.

LIFE SUCCESS SYSTEM: Seminars

Life Mastery 1: Million-Dollar Relationships (three days)

Success Mastery 1: Pursuit of Passion (three days)

Life Mastery 2: Live, Love, and Laugh (three days)

LIFE SUCCESS SYSTEM